U.S. Department of Transportation
Federal Aviation Administration

T0007691

FAA-S-ACS-1
FAA-G-ACS-1

Airman Certification Standards

Aviation Mechanic

General, Airframe, and Powerplant

AVIATION SUPPLIES & ACADEMICS, INC.
NEWCASTLE, WASHINGTON

Aviation Mechanic General, Airframe, and Powerplant Airman Certification Standards

Aviation Supplies & Academics, Inc.
7005 132nd Place SE
Newcastle, Washington 98059
asa@asa2fly.com | 425-235-1500 | asa2fly.com

Visit asa2fly.com/acsupdates for FAA revisions affecting this title.

None of the material in this book supersedes any operational documents or procedures issued by the Federal Aviation Administration.

ASA-ACS-1
ISBN 978-1-64425-275-8

Additional formats available:
eBook EPUB   ISBN 978-1-64425-276-5
eBook PDF   ISBN 978-1-64425-277-2

Printed in the United States of America

2026 2025 2024 2023 2022   9 8 7 6 5 4 3 2 1

FAA-G-ACS-1
Companion Guide to the Aviation Mechanic General, Airframe, and Powerplant Airman Certification Standards

FAA-S-ACS-1
Aviation Mechanic General, Airframe, and Powerplant Airman Certification Standards

I. General

II. Airframe

III. Powerplant

Appendix 1: Practical Test Roles, Responsibilities, and Outcomes

Appendix 2: Safety

U.S. Department
of Transportation

**Federal Aviation
Administration**

FAA-G-ACS-1

Companion Guide
to the
Aviation Mechanic General, Airframe, and
Powerplant Airman Certification Standards

Flight Standards Service
Washington, DC 20591

Foreword

The Federal Aviation Administration (FAA) developed FAA-G-ACS-1, Companion Guide to the Aviation Mechanic General, Airframe, and Powerplant Airman Certification Standards, to be used as a companion guide to FAA-S-ACS-1, Aviation Mechanic General, Airframe, and Powerplant Airman Certification Standards (ACS).

This guide contains information that may be used in concert with the regulatory material in the ACS and assists the applicant and examiner in preparing for the knowledge, oral, and practical tests.

This guide and the ACS are available for download from www.faa.gov.

Please send comments regarding this document using the following link to the Airman Testing Branch Mailbox (afs630comments@faa.gov).

Revision History

Document #	Description	Development Date
FAA-G-ACS-1	Companion Guide for Aviation Mechanic General, Airframe, and Powerplant Airman Certification Standards	May 2022

Introduction

Why We Created This Guide

The FAA created this guide to provide information on non-regulatory material regarding the FAA-S-ACS-1, Aviation Mechanic General, Airframe, and Powerplant Airman Certification Standards that is relevant and useful to the community. The regulatory material is found in the ACS.

The FAA notes that the Aviation Mechanic General, Airframe, and Powerplant Airman Certification Standards will be used as the testing standard for the written, oral, and practical tests after July 31, 2023. Therefore, this guidance will be applicable after July 31, 2023. Until July 31, 2023, the FAA will use the Aviation Mechanic General, Airframe, and Powerplant Practical Test Standards as the testing standard.

How This Guide Works with the ACS

The material in this guide is for informational purposes. The guide is designed to provide the applicant for a certificate or rating with test preparatory information. The guide also provides a list of references and abbreviations/acronyms that may be used throughout the ACS for study and research.

The material in this guide is non-regulatory and may contain terms, such as should or may.

- Should indicates actions that are recommended, but not regulatory.
- May is used in a permissive sense to state authority or permission to do the act prescribed.

This guidance is not legally binding in its own right and will not be relied upon by the FAA as a separate basis for affirmative enforcement action or other administrative penalty. Conformity with the guidance is voluntary only and nonconformity will not affect rights and obligations under existing statutes and regulations.

Airman Certification Standards Concept

The goal of the airman certification process is to ensure the applicant possesses knowledge, risk management, and basic skills consistent with the privileges of the certificate or rating being exercised. The ACS concept forms a more comprehensive standard for what an applicant knows, considers, and does for the safe conduct and successful completion of each subject to be tested on the knowledge (written) test and oral and practical tests. The FAA notes that while 14 CFR parts 65 and 147 use the term "written test," the FAA has historically used the terms "knowledge test" and "written test" in the context of airman certification testing interchangeably and continues to do so in this companion guide. Additionally, the terms "Mechanic" and "Aviation Maintenance Technician (AMT)" are used interchangeably in this document.

In fulfilling its responsibilities for the airman certification process, the FAA plans, develops, and maintains materials related to airman certification training and testing. The FAA written test measures the minimum standard of aeronautical knowledge required by Title 14 of the Code of Federal Regulations (14 CFR) part 65. Other materials, such as handbooks in the FAA-H-8083 series, provide information to applicants on aeronautical knowledge, risk management, and associated skills, including the knowledge and skill required to identify hazards and mitigate risks.

Safe operations on today's aircraft require integration of aeronautical knowledge, risk management, and skill standards. To accomplish these goals, the FAA draws upon the expertise of organizations and individuals across the aviation and training community to develop the ACS.

The ACS defines the elements of knowledge and skill for each airman certificate or rating defined in 14 CFR part 65, subpart D.

Through the oral and practical portion of the test, the FAA evaluators assess the applicant's application of the knowledge, risk management, and skill in the subject area. For some topics, the evaluator asks the applicant to describe or explain. For other items, the evaluator assesses the applicant's understanding by providing a scenario that requires the applicant to appropriately apply knowledge and demonstrate skills as required for the circumstances of the given scenario.

Note: As used in the ACS, an evaluator is any person authorized to conduct airman testing (e.g., an FAA Aviation Safety Inspector [ASI] or Designated Mechanic Examiner [DME]).

These procedures ensure that airman applicants meet a satisfactory level of competency and workmanship required for certification. Each applicant is required to demonstrate a minimum satisfactory competency level, regardless of their previous education or background, in order to obtain a certificate. All applicants for an FAA Aviation Mechanic Certificate must qualify by meeting the prescribed requirements as stated in 14 CFR part 65, section 65.77 (Experience requirements). They must additionally pass required written tests and the oral and practical tests for the certificate or rating(s) sought, in accordance with 14 CFR part 65, sections 65.75 (Knowledge requirements) and 65.79 (Skill requirements). The Aviation Mechanic General, Airframe, and Powerplant ACS is incorporated by reference into 14 CFR part 65 as the testing standard for each test after July 31, 2023. Additionally, the Aviation Mechanic General, Airframe, and Powerplant ACS is incorporated by reference into 14 CFR part 147, Aviation Maintenance Technician Schools (AMTS), as the training standard.

Chapter 1: Overview of Mechanic Testing Process

Overview

The Administrator of the FAA has the authority to issue airman certificates to individuals when the Administrator finds that the individual is qualified for and able to perform the duties related to the certificate pursuant to 49 USC 44703. 14 CFR part 65, subpart D – Mechanics, contains the qualification regulations to obtain a mechanic certificate. All applicants for an FAA Mechanic Certificate must qualify by meeting the experience requirements of 14 CFR part 65, section 65.77. After meeting the applicable experience requirements, applicants must pass a written test, appropriate to the rating sought, which covers the subject areas contained in ACS, pursuant to 14 CFR part 65, section 65.75. After passing each section of the written test, each applicant must pass an oral test and a practical test, as appropriate to the rating sought, by demonstrating the assigned objectives for the subject areas contained in the ACS, pursuant to 14 CFR part 65, section 65.79. Through the oral and practical portion of the test, the FAA assesses the applicant's application of the knowledge, risk management, and skill in the subject area.

These procedures ensure that airman applicants meet a satisfactory level of competency and workmanship required for certification. Each applicant is required to demonstrate a minimum satisfactory competency level, designated in the applicable section of the ACS, regardless of their previous education or background.

Evaluators must adhere to the applicable regulations and will follow applicable guidance when evaluating an applicant's test performance for an FAA Mechanic Certificate. This includes:

- 14 CFR part 65;
- FAA Order 8000.95 Designee Management Policy (applicable sections as revised);
- FAA Order 8900.2, General Aviation Airman Designee Handbook applicable sections (as revised);
- FAA Order 8900.1, Flight Standards Information Management System (FSIMS) (as revised); and
- FAA-S-ACS-1, Aviation Mechanic General, Airframe, and Powerplant Airman Certification Standards.

Mechanic Certificate Eligibility Requirements

To be eligible to be issued a mechanic certificate and rating(s), pursuant to 14 CFR part 65, section 65.71, an applicant must:

- Be at least 18 years of age;
- Be able to read, write, speak, and understand the English language (or in the case of an applicant who does not meet this requirement and who is employed outside of the U.S. by a U.S. air carrier, have the certificate endorsed "valid only outside the United States");
- Meet the applicable experience requirements of 14 CFR part 65, section 65.77 (i.e., the applicant must present to the FAA either an authenticated document from a certificated aviation maintenance technician school in accordance with14 CFR part 147, section 147.21, or documentary evidence, satisfactory to the Administrator, of the prescribed amount of practical experience);
- Pass a written test, appropriate to the rating sought, in accordance with14 CFR part 65, section 65.75;
- Pass an oral test and a practical test, as appropriate to the rating sought, in accordance with14 CFR part 65, section 65.79; and
- Comply with the applicable sections of 14 CFR part 65, subpart D.

Pursuant to 14 CFR part 65, section 65.75(b), the applicant must pass the applicable written tests before applying for the oral and practical tests, unless the applicant is a student of a 14 CFR part 147 Aviation Maintenance Technician School (AMTS) and has been approved by the FAA to test under 14 CFR part 65, section 65.80.

In accordance with 14 CFR part 65, section 65.71(a)(3), the applicant must have passed all of the prescribed tests (i.e., written, oral, and practical) for the rating sought, within a period of 24 months.

Applicants who otherwise cannot meet certification requirements may submit a petition for exemption from the applicable regulation in accordance with 14 CFR part 11. FAA field offices do not issue exemptions. A grant of exemption is not guaranteed.

Testing under 14 CFR part 65, section 65.80

14 CFR part 65, section 65.80 permits an applicant who is a student of an AMTS to take the oral and practical tests prior to the written tests if an AMTS shows to an FAA inspector that the applicant has made satisfactory progress at the school and is prepared to take the oral and practical tests.

Authorization for AMTS Students to Take General Written Test Early (14 CFR part 65, section 65.75(c))

Pursuant to 14 CFR part 65, section 65.75(c), applicants who are students of an AMTS may take the mechanic general written test prior to meeting the applicable experience requirements of 14 CFR part 65, section 65.77 provided the applicant presents an authenticated document from an AMTS that demonstrates satisfactory completion of the general portion of the school's curriculum and specifies the completion date.

Note: While an AMTS is required to provide an authenticated document to each graduating student, which can be utilized to meet the experience requirements of 14 CFR part 65, section 65.77, an AMTS is not required to provide authenticated documentation that demonstrates satisfactory completion of the general portion of the school's curriculum. The FAA notes that if the AMTS does not issue such a document, then the student will not be eligible to take the general written test early.

Aviation English Language Standard

In accordance with the requirements of 14 CFR part 65, section 65.71, and the FAA Aviation English Language Proficiency Standard, the applicant must demonstrate the ability to read, write, speak, and understand the English language throughout the application and testing process. English language proficiency is required. Normal restatement of questions as would be done for a native English speaker is permitted and does not constitute grounds for disqualification. Additional information may be found in Advisory Circular 60-28, FAA English Language Standard for an FAA Certificate Issued Under 14 CFR Part 61, 63, 65, and 107, as revised.

Applicant Misconduct During Written Testing

To avoid test compromise, airman knowledge testing centers follow strict security procedures established by the FAA. The FAA has directed testing centers to terminate a test anytime a proctor suspects a cheating incident has occurred.

No person who commits a prohibited act is eligible for any airman certificate or added rating for a period of 1 year after the date of that act, pursuant to 14 CFR part 65, section 65.18. In addition, the commission of that act is a basis for suspending or revoking any airman certificate or rating held by that person.

Requests for Special Accommodations

Applicants may request a special accommodation for their written test through the testing center test registration and scheduling process. The process allows the applicant to select the specific accommodation that meets the specific need in accordance with the Americans with Disabilities Act of 1990 (ADA). Requests for special accommodations are asked to include:

- a copy of medical documentation, including the diagnosing physician's name and contact information, verifying the applicant has condition requiring a special accommodation; and
- the requested method of test administration.

Passing Grade

Pursuant to 14 CFR part 65, section 65.17, the minimum passing grade for each test is 70 percent.

Retests

An applicant for a written, oral, or practical test for a certificate or rating, or for an additional rating under 14 CFR part 65, may apply for retesting in accordance with 14 CFR part 65, section 65.19.

Retests do not require a 30-day waiting period if the applicant presents a signed statement from an airman holding the certificate and rating(s) sought by the applicant certifying that the airman has given the applicant additional instruction in each of the subjects failed and that the airman considers the applicant ready for retesting.

After a 30-day waiting period for retesting, a signed statement of additional training is not required.

Chapter 2: How to Use the ACS

Evaluators must conduct practical tests in accordance with the appropriate ACS and policies set forth in the current version of FAA Order 8900.1, Flight Standards Information Management System.

The ACS consists of three Sections: **General, Airframe, and Powerplant**.

Each Section includes *Subjects* appropriate to that Section and consistent with the expertise necessary to obtain a mechanic certificate under 14 CFR part 65.

Each Subject begins with an *Objective* stating what the applicant should know, consider, and do, as appropriate. The ACS then lists the aeronautical knowledge, risk management, and skill elements relevant to the specific Subjects, along with the conditions and standards for acceptable performance.

- **Knowledge**—(written test, oral test) elements are indicated by use of the words, "Exhibits knowledge in..."

- **Risk**—(oral test, practical test) elements are indicated by the use of the words, "Determine, Identify, Creates..."

- **Skill**—(practical test) elements are indicated by the use of the words, "Demonstrates the skill to perform..."

The ACS may use *Notes* to emphasize special considerations. The ACS uses the terms "will" and "must" to convey directive (mandatory) information. The term "may" is used in a permissive sense to state authority or permission to do the act prescribed.

Element codes in the ACS divide into four components. For example,

AM.I.A.K1:

    AM = ACS (Aviation Mechanic)

    I = Section (General)

    A = Subject (Basic Electricity)

    K1 = Knowledge Element (Electron theory (conventional flow vs. electron flow.))

Knowledge test questions are linked to the ACS codes, which replace the previous system of Learning Statement Codes (LSC). After this transition, the AKTR will list an ACS code that correlates to a specific Subject element for a given Section and Subject. This will allow remedial instruction and re-testing to be specific and based on explicit learning criteria.

The FAA encourages applicants and instructors to use the ACS when preparing for tests.

Chapter 3: Written Test Description

Written Test Description

The written test is an important part of the airman certification process and is developed in accordance with the Aviation Mechanic General, Airframe, and Powerplant Airman Certification Standards as incorporated by reference into14 CFR part 65, section 65.75. Applicants must pass the written tests before taking the oral and practical tests (except when testing under the provision of 14 CFR part 65, section 65.80). Written tests are effective instruments for aviation safety and regulation measurement. However, these tests can only sample the vast amount of knowledge every AMT needs to know.

The written test consists of objective multiple-choice questions. There is a single correct response for each test question. Each test question is independent of the other questions. A correct response to one question does not depend on or influence the correct response to another.

There are three Aviation Maintenance Technician Written Tests:

Written Test Code	Test Name	# of Questions	Age	Hours	Passing Score
AMG	Aviation Mechanic Technician - General	60	N/A	2.0	70
AMA	Aviation Mechanic Technician - Airframe	100	N/A	2.0	70
AMP	Aviation Mechanic Technician - Powerplant	100	N/A	2.0	70

Authorization To Take a Written Test.

An airman applicant may present one or more of the following item(s) to an Airman Knowledge Testing Center to show authorization to take an AMT (mechanic) test:

- An authenticated document from an AMTS. The document must contain the information required by 14 CFR part 147, section 147.21. The completed curriculum as indicated on the document authorizes the applicant to take the corresponding test (i.e., either general and airframe; general and powerplant; or general, airframe, and powerplant).
- An original FAA Form 8610-2, Airman Certificate and/or Rating Application, attesting to practical experience. Block V must be signed and completed by an FAA Flight Standards inspector.
- Joint Services Aviation Maintenance Technician Certification Council (JSAMTCC) Military Certificate of Eligibility attesting to practical experience. The completed curriculum as indicated on the certificate authorizes the applicant to take the corresponding test (i.e., either general and airframe; general and powerplant; or general, airframe, and powerplant).
- If taking a retest, a previously issued AKTR with failed test results.

Note: In all instances, the applicant should retain their original document(s). The testing center will make a copy of the document for their records.

Authorization for AMTS students to Take General Written Test Early.

Pursuant to 14 CFR part 65, section 65.75(c), an applicant may take the mechanic general written test prior to meeting the applicable experience requirements of 14 CFR part 65, section 65.77. The applicant must present an authenticated document from an AMTS that demonstrates satisfactory completion of the general portion of the school's curriculum and specifies the completion date.

Written Test Blueprints

The following charts show what percentage of each subject area an applicant can expect to see on their written tests.

Note: FAA written tests contain topics that include the maintenance, repair, alteration, inspection of aviation products, and relevant FAA regulations.

Aviation Mechanic – General   *60-Question Test*

AMG Knowledge Areas	Percentage of Test Questions by Knowledge Area
Fundamentals of Electricity and Electronics	5 - 15%
Aircraft Drawings	5 - 10%
Weight and Balance	5 - 10%
Fluid Lines and Fittings	5 - 10%
Aircraft Materials, Hardware, and Processes	5 - 10%
Ground Operations and Servicing	5 - 15%
Cleaning and Corrosion Control	5 - 10%
Mathematics	5 - 10%
Regulations, Maintenance Forms, Records, and Publications	5 - 10%
Physics for Aviation	5 - 10%
Inspection Concepts and Techniques	5 - 10%
Human Factors	5 - 10%

Aviation Mechanic – Airframe   *100-Question Test*

AMA Knowledge Areas	Percentage of Test Questions by Knowledge Area
Metallic Structures	5 - 15%
Non-Metallic Structures	5 - 10%
Flight Controls	5 - 10%
Airframe Inspection	5 - 15%
Landing Gear Systems	5 - 10%
Hydraulic and Pneumatic Systems	5 - 10%
Environmental Systems	5 - 10%
Aircraft Instrument Systems	5 - 10%
Communication, Light Signals, and Runway Lighting Systems	5 - 10%
Aircraft Fuel Systems	5 - 10%
Aircraft Electrical Systems	5 - 10%
Ice and Rain Control Systems	5 - 10%
Airframe Fire Protection Systems	5 - 10%

AMA Knowledge Areas	Percentage of Test Questions by Knowledge Area
Rotorcraft Fundamentals	5 - 10%
Water and Waste Systems	5 - 10%

Aviation Mechanic – Powerplant   *100-Question Test*

AMP Knowledge Areas	Percentage of Test Questions by Knowledge Area
Reciprocating Engines	5 - 15%
Turbine Engines	5 - 10%
Engine Inspection	5 - 10%
Engine Instrument Systems	5 - 10%
Engine Fire Protection Systems	5 - 10%
Engine Electrical Systems	5 - 15%
Engine Lubrication Systems	5 - 10%
Ignition and Starting Systems	5 - 10%
Engine Fuel and Fuel Metering Systems	5 - 10%
Reciprocating Engine Induction and Cooling Systems	5 - 10%
Turbine Engine Air Systems	5 - 10%
Engine Exhaust and Reverser Systems	5 - 10%
Propellers	5 - 10%

Chapter 4: How to Register for an FAA Airman Knowledge Test

14 CFR part 65, section 65.11, provides that application for a certificate and/or rating must be made on a form and in a manner prescribed by the Administrator. As part of the application process, the FAA utilizes the testing vendor PSI Services, LLC (PSI). Registering to take an FAA Airman Knowledge Test is an easy process that can be done online or over the phone with PSI in just a few simple steps.

Note: The PSI Testing procedures are standardized to apply to all airman knowledge testing (e.g., pilots, mechanics, dispatchers, etc.), which is referred to as the "written test" in applicable aviation mechanic regulations. Therefore, where this guidance document utilizes the phrase "Airman Knowledge Test" in this section, it should be understood that the FAA is referring to the aviation mechanic written test for the purpose of meeting the knowledge requirements of 14 CFR part 65, section 65.75.

Step 1. Obtain an FAA Tracking Number

All airmen taking an FAA Airman Knowledge Test need to have an FAA tracking number (FTN) prior to taking any test. The FTN is easily obtained and only takes a few minutes.

Integrated Airman Certification and Rating Application (IACRA) is the web-based certification/rating application that guides the user through the FAA's airman application process for certification. To obtain an FTN, applicants will need to follow the instructions provided on the FAA's IACRA website located here: https://iacra.faa.gov/IACRA/Default.aspx.

The following video provides information about creating an IACRA account and obtaining an FTN. The specific instructions begin at the 14-minute mark in the video. https://www.youtube.com/watch?v=ETLsH8BruBM&feature=youtu.be.

Step 2. Create an Account with PSI

After obtaining the FTN, applicants will need to create an account with PSI. PSI is the professional testing company contracted with the FAA to administer all FAA Airman Knowledge Tests at approved PSI testing centers. PSI operates hundreds of testing centers that offer a full range of airman knowledge tests. For information on authorized airman knowledge testing centers and to register, schedule, and pay for the written test, visit https://faa.psiexams.com/faa/login. Using this link, an applicant can register for the respective airman knowledge test.

Step 3. Registration: Select Test and Testing Center

After obtaining an FTN and creating an account with PSI, applicants can schedule any knowledge test they are qualified to take. The PSI online system walks the applicant through the process of selecting a testing center in their area and choosing the specific knowledge (written) test they wish to take.

After the test and testing center are selected, the next step in the test scheduling process is for the applicant to select an available time slot to take the test at the selected testing center on the desired test date, then pay for the test.

Applicant Name Considerations for AKTR and the Mechanic Application Form

The name displayed on an Airman Knowledge Test Report (AKTR) is exactly how the applicant entered it when registering in IACRA and obtaining their FTN. The IACRA application sends basic information to the PSI test registration system verifying the applicant's FTN. The PSI test registration system does not allow an applicant to make changes to their name or correct any misspellings. If an applicant needs to make a correction to their name, it can be done within the IACRA application, then refreshed in the PSI system when the applicant logs in again.

If an incorrect middle initial, spelling variant, or different middle name is on the AKTR, or if the AKTR has a first name variation of any kind, the evaluator for the practical test will attach an explanation to the IACRA or paper application. If the last name on the AKTR has a different spelling or suffix, an IACRA application is not possible. The applicant will complete a paper application and the evaluator will include an explanation to avoid a correction notice.

At the Test Center

When at the test center on the day of the test, the applicant provides proper identification. An acceptable identification document includes a recent photograph, date of birth, signature, and actual residential address, if different from the mailing address. This information may be presented in more than one form of identification. Acceptable forms of identification include, but are not limited to, driver's licenses, government identification cards, passports, alien residency (green) cards, and military identification cards. Information on acceptable forms of identification is available at www.faa.gov/training_testing/testing.

Applicants also need to present their authorization to test; refer to Chapter 3 of this guide. Information on acceptable forms of authorization is also available at www.faa.gov/training_testing/testing.

The applicant retains all original forms/documents. The proctor will make a photocopy of the certificate presented at the time of applicant processing and returns the original documents to the applicant.

Note: Before starting the actual test, the testing center provides an opportunity to practice navigating through the test. This practice or tutorial session may include sample questions to familiarize the applicant with the look and feel of the software (e.g., selecting an answer, marking a question for later review, monitoring time remaining for the test, and other features of the testing software). PSI also provides sample tests for registered users on their website: https://faa.psiexams.com/faa/login.

Acceptable and Unacceptable Materials

Except as authorized by the Administrator under 14 CFR part 65, section 65.18, no person may use any material or aid during the period that the test is being given. The following table describes acceptable and unacceptable aids, reference materials, and test materials if the material does not include actual test questions or answers:

Acceptable Materials	Unacceptable Materials	Notes
Supplement book provided by the proctor	Written materials that are handwritten, printed, or electronic	Testing centers may provide calculators and/or deny the use of personal calculators.
All models of aviation-oriented calculators or small electronic calculators that perform only arithmetic functions	Electronic calculators incorporating permanent or continuous type memory circuits without erasure capability	Proctor may prohibit the use of an applicant's calculator if the proctor is unable to determine the calculator's erasure capability
Calculators with simple programmable memories, which allow the addition to, subtraction from, or retrieval of one number from the memory, or simple functions, such as square root and percentages	Magnetic Cards, magnetic tapes, modules, computer chips, or any other device upon which pre-written programs or information related to the test can be stored and retrieved	Printouts of data should be surrendered at the completion of the test if the calculator incorporates this design feature

Acceptable Materials	Unacceptable Materials	Notes
Scales, straightedges, protractors, plotters, navigation computers, blank log sheets, holding pattern entry aids, and electronic or mechanical calculators that are directly related to the test	Dictionaries	Before, and upon completion of the test, while in the presence of the proctor, actuate the ON/OFF switch or RESET button, and perform any other function that ensures erasure of any data stored in memory circuits
Manufacturer's permanently inscribed instructions on the front and back of such aids (e.g., formulas, conversions, regulations, signals, weather data, holding pattern diagrams, frequencies, weight and balance formulas, and air traffic control procedures)	Any booklet or manual containing instructions related to the use of test aids	Proctor makes the final determination regarding aids, reference materials, and test materials

Test Tips

- Carefully read the instructions provided with the test.
- Answer each question in accordance with the current regulations and guidance publications.
- Read each question carefully before looking at the answer options. You should clearly understand the problem before trying to solve it.
- After formulating a response, determine which answer option corresponds with your answer. The answer you choose should completely solve the problem.
- Remember that only one answer is complete and correct. The other possible answers are either incomplete or erroneous.
- If a certain question is difficult for you, mark it for review and return to it after you have answered the less difficult questions. This procedure will enable you to use the available time to maximum advantage.
- When solving a calculation problem, be sure to read all the associated notes.
- For questions involving the use of a graph, you may request a printed copy that you can mark in computing your answer. This copy and all other notes and paperwork should be given to the testing center upon completion of the test.

Cheating or Other Unauthorized Conduct

The FAA prohibits cheating and unauthorized conduct on written tests, in accordance with 14 CFR part 65, section 65.18. To avoid test compromise, computer testing centers follow procedures established with the FAA. The FAA has directed testing centers to terminate a test at any time a proctor suspects that a cheating incident has occurred.

The FAA will investigate any alleged incident of cheating and any airman certificate or rating held may be suspended or revoked if the agency determines that cheating or unauthorized conduct has occurred. No person who commits a prohibited act is eligible for any airman or ground instructor certificate or rating for a period of 1 year after the date of that act (see 14 CFR part 65, section 65.18(b)).

Testing Procedures for Applicants Requesting Special Accommodations

Applicants may request a special accommodation for their airman knowledge test through the PSI test registration and scheduling process. The PSI special accommodations team will work with the applicant and the desired testing center to ensure the accommodation(s) are set up on test day. The applicant should be prepared to provide medical documentation to the PSI special accommodations team for verification.

Chapter 5: Airman Knowledge Test Report (AKTR)

Upon completion of the written test, the applicant receives a printed AKTR documenting the score. The applicant should retain the original AKTR. Prior to taking the practical test, the applicant presents the original AKTR to the evaluator. The evaluator will assess any noted areas of deficiency during the oral portion of the practical test.

An AKTR expires 24 calendar months after the month the applicant completes the written test pursuant to 14 CFR part 65, section 65.71(a)(3) and (b). If the AKTR expires before completion of the practical test, the applicant must retake, pass, and present the AKTR in order to start or continue the practical test.

Replacement test reports for knowledge tests taken **on or before January 10, 2020**, may be obtained from the FAA. The form to request a replacement test report and additional information may be found at https://www.faa.gov/licenses_certificates/airmen_certification/test_results_replacement.

For tests taken **on or after January 13, 2020**, an AKTR may be reprinted from: https://faa.psiexams.com/faa/login, free of charge.

For additional questions, call the Airmen Certification Branch Toll Free: (866) 878-2498.

FAA Written Test Question Coding

As discussed in chapter 2 of this guide, the system of ACS codes is replacing the system of LSC on an AKTR. Written tests taken as of the effective date of this ACS will list an ACS code for each missed question that correlates to a specific Subject element for a given Section and Subject. This change enables specific and targeted remedial instruction and retesting based on specified learning criteria. Each ACS code is tied to a unique Subject element in the ACS itself. Refer to Chapter 2 for a description of the coding used on the knowledge test report.

Missed Knowledge Test Questions

As part of the oral portion of the oral and practical tests, applicants will be subject to retesting on the subjects identified by the codes shown on the AKTR.

Chapter 6: The Oral and Practical (O&P) Test Process

Each applicant for a Mechanic Certificate must successfully pass a written test, an oral test, and a practical test to comply with the general eligibility requirements to obtain a mechanic certificate or rating (see14 CFR part 65, section 65.53). The O&P tests are typically conducted by an FAA DME; however, in some circumstances, an FAA inspector may conduct an oral and/or practical test.

14 CFR part 65, section 65.11, provides that application for a certificate and/or rating must be made on a form and in a manner prescribed by the Administrator. As part of the application process, the applicant must contact a DME in order to schedule the O&P tests. A list of DMEs is available at www.faa.gov or from a local Flight Standards Office.

Prior to the tests, the evaluator conducts a pre-test interview with the applicant. This pre-test interview provides the evaluator and applicant with information needed for the test, such as the date, time, and location of the test. It also establishes a testing schedule and allows the evaluator to see any codes associated with the written test report and identify any deficient areas that should be included on the oral test. FAA designees may charge a reasonable fee for their services and this fee should be discussed and agreed upon prior to taking the scheduled test.

The applicant should bring the following documentation to the pre-test interview and the O&P test:

- Two identically-prepared FAA Forms 8610-2, Airman Certificate and/or Rating Application, with original signatures;
- Unless early testing under 14 CFR part 65, section 65.80, written test results indicating a passing grade, applicable to the appropriate rating(s) sought ; and
- A current government-issued photo identification with a signature from the issuing official, such as a passport, U.S. Military ID, driver's license, etc.

Additionally, the applicant should bring the following eligibility documentation:

If testing on the basis of this eligibility:	The applicant should bring this documentation:
Graduation from an FAA certificated 14 CFR part 147 AMTS;	An authenticated document from an AMTS indicating the applicant's date of graduation and curriculum completed, applicable to the certificate or rating sought.
Civil or Military Practical experience as provided by14 CFR part 65, section 65.77;	A signature in Block V of FAA Form 8610-2 authorizing the applicant to test.
Practical experience through the JSAMTCC program;	A military certificate of eligibility, applicable to the certificate or rating sought.
Satisfactory progress at an FAA certificate 14 CFR part 147 AMTS pursuant to14 CFR part 65, section 65.80;	A signature in Section II of FAA Form 8610-2 from a school official and FAA inspector authorizing the applicant to test.

Failure to bring the required documents to the pre-test interview or O&P tests may result in the test being delayed or terminated.

Note: An evaluator conducts oral or practical tests with no more than one applicant at a time.

Missed Questions From Written Test

The oral portion of the O&P tests will consist of questions to retest any deficient knowledge areas from the FAA written tests. Applicants should expect to be questioned on the topics associated with the codes displayed on the AKTR.

Applicant Responsibilities

Every applicant for a mechanic certificate is required to demonstrate their knowledge and skill to a minimum satisfactory level, regardless of their previous education, experience, or background, in accordance with the Aviation Mechanic General, Airframe, and Powerplant Airman Certification Standards as incorporated by reference into 14 CFR part 65, section 65.79.

The applicant is responsible for demonstrating acceptable knowledge of the established standards for knowledge, skill, and risk management elements in all subjects appropriate to the certificate and rating sought. The applicant should use the ACS and its references in preparation to take the oral and practical tests.

An applicant is not permitted to know before testing begins which selections from each subject area are to be included in their test. Therefore, an applicant should be well prepared in all knowledge, risk management, and skill elements included in the ACS.

The oral portion of the tests consists of questions specific to the topics associated with the codes on the AKTR. Applicants must demonstrate acceptable knowledge of the subjects missed on the FAA knowledge test. If the applicant scores 100% on the written test, the oral test will consist of a minimum number of randomly selected oral questions. During the oral portion of the test the applicant is NOT allowed to use any reference material to answer the oral questions asked by the examiner.

The practical (i.e., skill) portion of the test is composed of practical projects and practical questioning specific to the projects being tested. The applicant may use reference materials to answer the practical questions asked during the practical projects portion of the test.

Note: Additional information for evaluators regarding the conduct of oral and practical tests is contained in the current revision of FAA Order 8900.1 or FAA Order 8900.2, as applicable.

All applicants must demonstrate an approval for return to service standard, where applicable, and demonstrate the ability to locate and apply the required reference materials. In instances where an approval for return to service standard cannot be achieved, the applicant must explain why the return to service standard was not met (e.g., when tolerances are outside of a product's limitations).

The practical portion of the tests are significant because they measure the applicant's ability to logically think and objectively apply their knowledge, while demonstrating the physical skills that enable them to carry out aircraft maintenance in a safe manner. Satisfactory demonstration of each skill tested is evidence the applicant meets the acceptable degree of competency for the certificate or rating sought.

AMT applicants meeting the experience requirements of 14 CFR part 65 should refer to 14 CFR part 65, section 65.77; they may be eligible to take the airman knowledge test for the general, airframe, and powerplant knowledge tests without any additional formal training (i.e., graduation from an ATMS).

Evaluator Responsibilities

The evaluator will ask the applicant to provide the AKTRs prior to generating the test. The evaluator then generates a complete test with a planning sheet to conduct the oral and practical tests. The evaluator includes all the questions and projects obtained from the internet-based Mechanic Test Generator (MTG).

The MTG includes oral questions from the knowledge elements of the ACS to retest those topics missed on the FAA knowledge tests, which will be asked during the oral portion of the test. If the applicant scores 100 percent on the written test, a minimum number of questions are asked during the oral test. The applicant is not permitted to use any reference material during the oral portion of the test.

The MTG also includes questions on the knowledge and risk management elements of the ACS, specific to the selected projects; these will be asked in context during the practical demonstration portion of the test. The applicant is allowed to use reference material for those questions that are given as part of the practical demonstration portion of the test. For this reason, the examiner will ensure that the oral and practical portions of the tests are kept separate. The evaluator administering the oral and practical tests will not combine subjects/elements during testing.

The test provided by the MTG contains questions, answers, projects, and performance standards for all elements of the oral and practical tests and is specific to the applicant. Although the tests are not provided to the applicant, it contains certain information in parentheses. This information is additional or clarifying information for the examiner. It is not expected that the applicant will recite all the information in parentheses, however, this information is acceptable as an alternative to what is stated in the answer.

The evaluator will personally observe all practical projects performed by the applicant. The practical portion of the test includes an ongoing evaluation of knowledge and risk management while evaluating the skill. The evaluator who conducts the practical test is responsible for determining that the applicant meets acceptable standards of knowledge and skill in the assigned subject areas. Every applicant is required to demonstrate a minimum satisfactory competency level, regardless of their previous educational background.

The following terms may be reviewed with the applicant prior to or during element assignment:

- **Inspect** means to examine (with or without inspection enhancing tools/equipment).
- **Check** means to verify proper operation.
- **Troubleshoot** means to analyze and identify malfunctions.
- **Service** means to perform functions that assure continued operation.
- **Repair** means to correct a defective condition and repair of an airframe or powerplant system including component replacement and adjustment.
- **Overhaul** means to disassemble, clean, inspect, repair as necessary, and reassemble.

Since an evaluator does not provide applicants with the selections in each subject area to be tested before the test begins, all applicants should be well prepared in all knowledge, risk management, and skill elements included in the ACS.

Further information regarding the requirements for conducting a practical test is contained in the current revision of FAA Order 8900.1 or FAA Order 8900.2, as applicable.

Required Material for the Practical Test

The evaluator shall provide all tools, equipment, and reference materials to support the test. These materials shall include, but are not limited to, 14 CFR, Airworthiness Directives, Advisory Circulars, manufacturer's technical and parts manuals, service information, and any other instructions and/or reference materials that are necessary to meet the performance standard of the assigned project.

All reference material shall be unmarked and in good condition.

The applicant's use of other reference material that the evaluator has NOT provided is prohibited. Use of nonprogrammable calculators is permitted where appropriate. Applicants may only use personal tools and equipment at the discretion of the evaluator.

Safety

Safety is a prime consideration at all times. The evaluator and applicant should be alert for hazards while performing any maintenance or troubleshooting projects. Should any project require an action that would jeopardize safety, the evaluator may ask the applicant to simulate that portion of the project.

The evaluator must ensure the applicant follows all safety recommendations/precautions while performing the assigned projects including, but not limited to, the following:

- Approach to the project; proper information and tools; preparation of the equipment; and observation of safety precautions such as wearing safety glasses, hearing protection, and any other required personal protective equipment (PPE).
- Cleaning, preparing, and protecting parts; skill in handling tools; thoroughness and cleanliness.
- Use of current maintenance and overhaul publications and procedures.
- Application of appropriate rules, risk management, and safety assessments.
- Attitude toward safety, manufacturer's recommendations, and acceptable industry practices. The applicant should be aware that any disregard for safety is not tolerated and will result in a failure.

Chapter 7: Oral and Practical Test Results

Passing the Oral and Practical Tests

When an applicant has passed all required tests in the prescribed period of time and meets all other eligibility requirements, the applicant is eligible to be issued a Temporary Airman Certificate. The subsequent Certification paragraph provides additional information on temporary certificates.

When an applicant is under 18 and has passed all of the required tests, the applicant should hold their documentation until they turn 18. When the applicant turns 18, they may take their test results (AKTR and 8610-2(s)) to their local Flight Standards office or a DME to be issued their temporary certificate.

Failing the Oral and Practical Tests

When an applicant has failed the oral test or the practical test, the applicant must be retested if the applicant wishes to receive an airman certificate.

Not Tested

When an applicant is not tested in a subject area, applicable to the rating applied for, the evaluator will annotate appropriately the parts of the test that were not tested. This may occur if the test was unable to be completed for any reason. The applicant must subsequently be tested in the areas annotated as "not tested" if the applicant wishes to receive an airman certificate.

Retesting the Oral and Practical

Chapter 1 provides information related to general retesting requirements pursuant to 14 CFR part 65, section 65.19.

An applicant who applies for retesting of an oral or practical test must provide the evaluator with all previous FAA Form 8610-2s that annotate failure or "not tested" portions of a test. Additionally, the applicant must provide the passed AKTR(s). The annotated Form 8610-2s presented as authorization will be reviewed and returned to the applicant.

If the applicant is retesting the oral portion of the test, they will test the entire Section that was failed (General, Airframe, or Powerplant). Failed and untested projects will carry forward to the retest.

If the applicant is retesting the practical portion of the test, the applicant is retested on the failed projects, an additional project in the same subject area, and with any subject areas not tested on the previous test.

Certification

Typically, upon successful completion of the testing process, the applicant is issued a temporary airman certificate by the DME while the applicant's application and supplementary documents are reviewed. After such review and confirmation of eligibility, the FAA will process and issue the airman certificate and/or ratings (see 14 CFR part 65, section 65.13). The temporary certificate must be signed by the designee and the applicant in order for it to be valid. The temporary certificate is valid for 120 days from the date of issuance.

If the temporary certificate expires before the airman's certificate is issued, the airman should contact their local Flight Standards Office (or International Field Office if outside the U.S.).If the mechanic certificate is not received in 120 days, the airman should contact the Airmen Certification Branch via the following:

Toll free: 1-866-878-2498

Website: http://registry.faa.gov

Email: 9-AMC-AFS760-Airmen@faa.gov

Certification information line: 405-954-3261

Chapter 8: References

This ACS is based on the following 14 CFR parts, FAA publications, FAA guidance, and learning aid documents.

References	Titles
14 CFR	Title 14 of the Code of Federal Regulations
14 CFR part 43	Maintenance, Preventive Maintenance, Rebuilding, and Alteration
14 CFR part 45	Identification and Registration Marking
14 CFR part 65	Certification: Airmen Other Than Flight Crewmembers
14 CFR part 91	General Operating and Flight Rules
14 CFR part 147	Aviation Maintenance Technician Schools
AC 20-35	Tiedown Sense
AC 25.1455-1	Waste Water/Potable Water Drain System Certification Testing
AC 25-11	Electronic Flight Displays
AC 43-9	Maintenance Records
AC 43.13-1	Acceptable Methods, Techniques and Practices - Aircraft Inspection & Repair
AC 43.13-2	Acceptable Methods, Techniques and Practices - Aircraft Alterations
AC 43-215	Standardized Procedures for Performing Aircraft Magnetic Compass Calibration
AC 45-2	Identification and Registration Marking
AC 60-11	Test Aids and Materials that May be Used by Airman Knowledge Testing Applicants
AC 60-28	FAA English Language Standard for an FAA Certificate Issued Under 14 CFR Parts 61, 63, 65, and 107
AC 120-39	Hazards of Waste Water Ice Accumulation Separating from Aircraft in Flight
AC 150/5210-20	Ground Vehicle Operations to include Taxiing or Towing an Aircraft on Airports
FAA-H-8083-1	Aircraft Weight and Balance Handbook
FAA-H-8083-2	Risk Management Handbook
FAA-H-8083-25	Pilot's Handbook of Aeronautical Knowledge
FAA-H-8083-30	Aviation Maintenance Technician Handbook–General
FAA-H-8083-31	Aviation Maintenance Technician Handbook–Airframe (Volumes 1 and 2)
FAA-H-8083-32	Aviation Maintenance Technician–Powerplant (Volumes 1 and 2)
POH/AFM	Pilot's Operating Handbook/FAA-Approved Airplane Flight Manual

Note: *Users should reference the current edition of the reference documents listed above. The current edition of all FAA publications can be found at: www.faa.gov.*

Chapter 9: Abbreviations and Acronyms

Abbreviations and Acronyms

14 CFR	Title 14 of the Code of Federal Regulations
AC	Advisory Circular
AC	Alternating Current
ACARS	Aircraft Communication Addressing and Reporting System
ACS	Airman Certification Standards
AD	Airworthiness Directive
ADF	Automatic Direction Finder
ADS-B	Automatic Dependent Surveillance Broadcast
AELP	Aviation English Language Proficiency
AFS	Flight Standards Service
AIS	Audio Integration System
AKT	Airman Knowledge Test
AKTR	Airman Knowledge Test Report
AMA	Aviation Maintenance - Airframe
AMG	Aviation Maintenance - General
AMP	Aviation Maintenance - Powerplant
AMT	Aviation Maintenance Technician
AMTS	Aviation Maintenance Technician School
ASAP	Aviation Safety Action Program
ASI	Aviation Safety Inspector
ASRP	Aviation Safety Reporting Program
ASRS	Aviation Safety Reporting System
ATC	Air Traffic Control
CFR	Code of Federal Regulations
CG	Center of Gravity
CPC	Corrosion Preventative Compounds
CSD	Constant-Speed Drive
DC	Direct Current
DME	Designated Mechanic Examiner
DME	Distance Measuring Equipment
EGT	Exhaust Gas Temperature
ELT	Emergency Locator Transmitter
EPR	Engine Pressure Ratio
FAA	Federal Aviation Administration
FADEC	Full Authority Digital Engine Controls
FOD	Foreign Object Debris
FOQA	Flight Operational Quality Assurance
FSDO	Flight Standards District Office
GPS	Global Positioning System
GPWS	Ground Proximity Warning Systems
HF	High Frequency
ID	Identification
IDG	Integrated Drive Generator

Abbreviations and Acronyms (continued)

IFR	Instrument Flight Rules
ILS	Instrument Landing System
INS	Inertial Navigation System
JSAMTCC	Joint Services Aviation Maintenance Technician Certification Council
LOSA	Line Operations Safety Audit
LSC	Learning Statement Codes
MAC	Mean Aerodynamic Chord
MTG	Mechanic Test Generator
NDT	Nondestructive Testing
NiCad	Nickle-Cadmium (battery)
NVRAM	Nonvolatile Random Access Memory
O&P	Oral and Practical
ODA	Organization Designation Authorization
OK	Oklahoma
P.O.	Post Office
RA	Radio Altimeter
RAM	Random Access Memory
ROM	Read-Only Memory
RNAV	Area Navigation
RPM	Revolutions Per Minute
SATCOM	Satellite Communications
SDS	Safety Data Sheets
SFC	Specific Fuel Consumption
SMS	Safety Management System
STC	Supplemental Type Certificate
SUPS	Suspected Unapproved Parts
TCAS	Traffic Collision Avoidance System
TCDS	Type Certificate Data Sheet
TSO	Technical Standard Order
U.S.	United States of America

U.S. Department
of Transportation

**Federal Aviation
Administration**

FAA-S-ACS-1

Aviation Mechanic
General, Airframe, and Powerplant
Airman Certification Standards

November 1, 2021

The Administrator of the Federal Aviation Administration signed the interim final rule "Part 147, Aviation Maintenance Technician Schools" on March 9, 2022. The interim final rule incorporates this version of the Aviation Mechanic General, Airframe, and Powerplant Airman Certification Standards (FAA-S-ACS-1) by reference. For identification and document-control purposes, this ACS is dated November 1, 2021. However, this ACS is not enforceable until the effective date of the interim final rule. Upon publication, the interim final rule can be found on the Federal Register's website, www.federalregister.gov, and will direct the effective date of compliance with this ACS.

**Flight Standards Service
Washington, DC 20591**

Foreword

The U.S. Department of Transportation (DOT), Federal Aviation Administration (FAA), Office of Safety Standards, Regulatory Support Division, Airman Testing Standards Branch has published the Aviation Mechanic General, Airframe, and Powerplant Airman Certification Standards (ACS) to communicate the aeronautical knowledge, risk management, and proficiency standards for the Mechanic Certificate.

This ACS is available for download from www.faa.gov. Please send comments regarding this document using the following link to the Airman Testing Branch Mailbox (afs630@faa.gov).

Revision History

Document	Description	Revision Date
FAA-S-ACS-1	Aviation Mechanic - General, Airframe, and Powerplant Airman Certification Standards	11/01/2021

I. General
Subject A. Fundamentals of Electricity and Electronics

References	*AC 43.13-1; FAA-H-8083-30*
Objective	*The following knowledge, risk management, and skill elements are required for basic electricity and electronics.*
Knowledge	*The applicant demonstrates understanding of:*
AM.I.A.K1	Electron theory (conventional flow vs. electron flow).
AM.I.A.K2	Magnetism.
AM.I.A.K3	Capacitance in a circuit.
AM.I.A.K4	Inductance in a circuit.
AM.I.A.K5	Alternating current (AC) electrical circuits.
AM.I.A.K6	Direct current (DC) electrical circuits.
AM.I.A.K7	Electrical laws and theory.
AM.I.A.K7a	a. Ohm's Law
AM.I.A.K7b	b. Kirchhoff's Laws
AM.I.A.K7c	c. Watt's Law
AM.I.A.K7d	d. Faraday's Law
AM.I.A.K7e	e. Lenz's Law
AM.I.A.K7f	f. Right-hand motor rule
AM.I.A.K8	Electrical measurement tools, principles, and procedures.
AM.I.A.K9	Voltage.
AM.I.A.K9a	a. Regulation
AM.I.A.K10	Current.
AM.I.A.K11	Resistance.
AM.I.A.K11a	a. Impedance
AM.I.A.K11b	b. Resistance in series
AM.I.A.K11c	c. Resistance in parallel
AM.I.A.K11d	d. Total resistance
AM.I.A.K12	Power.
AM.I.A.K13	Series circuits.
AM.I.A.K14	Parallel circuits.
AM.I.A.K15	Aircraft batteries.
AM.I.A.K16	Transformers.
AM.I.A.K17	Circuit continuity.
AM.I.A.K18	Controlling devices, including switches and relays.
AM.I.A.K19	Protective devices, including fuses, circuit breakers, and current limiters.
AM.I.A.K20	Resistor types and color coding.
AM.I.A.K21	Semiconductors, including diodes, transistors, and integrated circuits.
AM.I.A.K22	Digital logic, including RAM, ROM, NVRAM, logic gates, inverter, rectifier, and flip flop.
AM.I.A.K23	Binary numbers.

AM.I.A.K24	Electrostatic discharge.
AM.I.A.K25	Electrical circuit drawings.
AM.I.A.K26	Complex/combined circuits.
AM.I.A.K27	AC and DC motors.
Risk Management	*The applicant demonstrates the ability to identify, assess, and mitigate risks associated with:*
AM.I.A.R1	Taking voltage, current, resistance, and capacitance measurements.
AM.I.A.R2	Handling, storage, and inspection of different types of batteries (i.e., lead acid, NiCad, lithium ion, gel cell).
AM.I.A.R3	High-voltage circuits (e.g., strobe lighting).
AM.I.A.R4	Working around batteries.
Skills	*The applicant demonstrates the ability to:*
AM.I.A.S1	Perform circuit continuity test.
AM.I.A.S2	Measure voltage.
AM.I.A.S3	Measure current.
AM.I.A.S4	Measure resistance.
AM.I.A.S5	Test a switch or relay.
AM.I.A.S6	Test a fuse or circuit breaker.
AM.I.A.S7	Read and interpret aircraft electrical circuit diagrams, and symbols, including solid state devices and logic functions.
AM.I.A.S8	Troubleshoot a circuit.
AM.I.A.S9	Identify symbols used in electrical and electronic schematic diagrams (e.g., grounds, shields, resistors, capacitors, fuses, circuit breakers, batteries, diodes, transistors, and integrated circuits).
AM.I.A.S10	Demonstrate how to test for short-circuit and open-circuit conditions.
AM.I.A.S11	Measure voltage drop across a resistor.
AM.I.A.S12	Determine or measure for open electrical circuits.
AM.I.A.S13	Inspect an aircraft battery.
AM.I.A.S14	Service an aircraft battery.

I. General

Subject B. Aircraft Drawings

References	*AC 43.13-1; FAA-H-8083-30*
Objective	*The following knowledge, risk management, and skill elements are required for aircraft drawings.*
Knowledge	*The applicant demonstrates understanding of:*
AM.I.B.K1	Drawings, blueprints, sketches, charts, graphs, and system schematics, including commonly used lines, symbols, and terminology.
AM.I.B.K2	Repair or alteration of an aircraft system or component(s) using drawings, blueprints, or system schematics to determine whether it conforms to its type design.
AM.I.B.K3	Inspection of an aircraft system or component(s) using drawings, blueprints, or system schematics.
AM.I.B.K4	Terms used in conjunction with aircraft drawings, blueprints, or system schematics.
Risk Management	*The applicant demonstrates the ability to identify, assess, and mitigate risks associated with:*
AM.I.B.R1	Interpretation of plus or minus tolerances as depicted on aircraft drawings.
AM.I.B.R2	Specifications for design of alterations and repairs.
AM.I.B.R3	Applicability of the drawing or schematic to the particular aircraft by model and serial number.
AM.I.B.R4	Identification of the current version and applicability of drawing being used.
Skills	*The applicant demonstrates the ability to:*
AM.I.B.S1	Draw a sketch of a repair or alteration.
AM.I.B.S2	Identify the meaning of lines and symbols used in an aircraft drawing.
AM.I.B.S3	Interpret dimensions used in an aircraft drawing.
AM.I.B.S4	Identify changes on an aircraft drawing.
AM.I.B.S5	Determine material requirements from an aircraft drawing.
AM.I.B.S6	Interpret graphs and charts.

I. General

Subject C. Weight and Balance

References	*AC 43.13-1; FAA-H-8083-1, FAA-H-8083-30*
Objective	*The following knowledge, risk management, and skill elements are required for weight and balance.*
Knowledge	*The applicant demonstrates understanding of:*
AM.I.C.K1	Weight and balance terminology.
AM.I.C.K2	Purpose for weighing an aircraft.
AM.I.C.K3	Weighing procedures, including the general preparations for weighing, with emphasis on aircraft weighing area considerations.
AM.I.C.K4	Procedures for calculation of the following: arm, positive or negative moment, center of gravity (CG), or moment index.
AM.I.C.K5	Purpose and application of weight and CG limits.
AM.I.C.K6	Purpose of determining CG.
AM.I.C.K7	Adverse loading considerations and how to calculate if adverse loading causes an out-of-limit condition.
AM.I.C.K8	Determine proper empty weight configuration.
AM.I.C.K9	Proper ballast placement.
AM.I.C.K10	Jacking an aircraft.
Risk Management	*The applicant demonstrates the ability to identify, assess, and mitigate risks associated with:*
AM.I.C.R1	Situations and conditions when jacking an aircraft.
AM.I.C.R2	Aircraft weighing procedures.
AM.I.C.R3	Use of scales.
AM.I.C.R4	Aerodynamic effect of CG that is forward or aft of CG limits.
AM.I.C.R5	Aerodynamic and performance effects of weight in excess of limits.
Skills	*The applicant demonstrates the ability to:*
AM.I.C.S1	Research and explain the procedures for weighing an aircraft.
AM.I.C.S2	Perform weight and balance calculations.
AM.I.C.S3	Calculate ballast weight shift and required weight location.
AM.I.C.S4	Check aircraft weighing scales for calibration.
AM.I.C.S5	Calculate weight and balance for an aircraft after an equipment change.
AM.I.C.S6	Compute forward and aft loaded CG limit.
AM.I.C.S7	Create a maintenance record for a weight and balance change.
AM.I.C.S8	Compute the empty weight and empty weight CG of an aircraft.
AM.I.C.S9	Calculate the moment of an item of equipment.
AM.I.C.S10	Identify tare items.
AM.I.C.S11	Locate weight and balance information.
AM.I.C.S12	Locate datum.
AM.I.C.S13	Locate weight and balance placarding and limitation requirements for an aircraft.
AM.I.C.S14	Revise an aircraft equipment list after equipment change.
AM.I.C.S15	Calculate the change needed to correct an out of balance condition.

| AM.I.C.S16 | Determine an aircraft's CG range using aircraft specifications, Type Certificate Data Sheets (TCDSs), and aircraft listings. |
| AM.I.C.S17 | Calculate a weight change and complete required records. |

Subject D. Fluid Lines and Fittings

References	*AC 43.13-1; FAA-H-8083-30*
Objective	*The following knowledge, risk management, and skill elements are required for fluid lines and fittings.*
Knowledge	*The applicant demonstrates understanding of:*
AM.I.D.K1	Tubing and hose materials, applications, sizes, and fittings.
AM.I.D.K2	Rigid line or flexible hose material identification.
AM.I.D.K3	Rigid line fabrication, installation, and inspection techniques/practices.
AM.I.D.K4	Flexible hose fabrication, installation, and inspection techniques/practices.
AM.I.D.K5	Importance of using a torque wrench when securing fluid hose and line fittings.
AM.I.D.K6	Use of torque seal or similar witness techniques after installing critical fluid hose and line fittings.
Risk Management	*The applicant demonstrates the ability to identify, assess, and mitigate risks associated with:*
AM.I.D.R1	System configuration prior to and during maintenance.
AM.I.D.R2	Use of required safety equipment.
AM.I.D.R3	Hazardous fluids.
AM.I.D.R4	High-pressure fluid systems.
AM.I.D.R5	A twisted hose.
AM.I.D.R6	A loosened fitting or a hose that has moved out of position.
AM.I.D.R7	Use of tools while applying torque to a fluid line.
Skills	*The applicant demonstrates the ability to:*
AM.I.D.S1	Fabricate a rigid line with a flare and a bend.
AM.I.D.S2	Install an aircraft rigid line.
AM.I.D.S3	Install an aircraft flexible hose.
AM.I.D.S4	Perform a rigid line or flexible hose inspection.
AM.I.D.S5	Identify installation and security requirements for rigid lines and flexible hoses.
AM.I.D.S6	Identify fluid lines, pneumatic lines, and fittings.
AM.I.D.S7	Fabricate a flexible hose.
AM.I.D.S8	Fabricate a flareless-fitting-tube connection.

I. General
Subject E. Aircraft Materials, Hardware, and Processes

References	AC 43.13-1; FAA-H-8083-30
Objective	The following knowledge, risk management, and skill elements are required for materials, hardware, and processes.
Knowledge	The applicant demonstrates understanding of:
AM.I.E.K1	Materials commonly used in aircraft and their general application.
AM.I.E.K2	Heat treatment and metal working processes.
AM.I.E.K3	Forces placed on aircraft materials (e.g., tension, compression, torsion, bending, strain, and shear).
AM.I.E.K4	Hardware commonly used in aircraft (e.g., bolts, nuts, screws, pins, washers, turnlock fasteners, cables, cable fittings, and rigid line couplings).
AM.I.E.K5	Safety wire and safety clip requirements and techniques.
AM.I.E.K6	Precision measurement tools, principles, and procedures.
AM.I.E.K7	Soldering preparation, types of solder, and flux usage.
AM.I.E.K8	Torquing tools, principles, and procedures.
AM.I.E.K9	Suitability and compatibility of materials and hardware used for maintenance.
AM.I.E.K10	Relationship between torque and fastener preload.
AM.I.E.K11	Identification markings on materials and hardware.
AM.I.E.K12	Characteristics of acceptable welds.
AM.I.E.K13	Characteristics of unacceptable welds.
AM.I.E.K14	Procedures for weld repairs.
Risk Management	The applicant demonstrates the ability to identify, assess, and mitigate risks associated with:
AM.I.E.R1	Use of personal protective equipment (PPE).
AM.I.E.R2	Improper torque.
AM.I.E.R3	Used hardware or suspected unapproved parts (SUPS).
AM.I.E.R4	Torquing techniques on critical, highly-stressed fasteners.
Skills	The applicant demonstrates the ability to:
AM.I.E.S1	Install safety wire on nuts, bolts, and turnbuckles.
AM.I.E.S2	Determine and properly torque aircraft hardware.
AM.I.E.S3	Inspect and check welds.
AM.I.E.S4	Identify aircraft materials and hardware based on manufacturer's markings.
AM.I.E.S5	Select and install aircraft bolts.
AM.I.E.S6	Make precision measurements with an instrument that has a Vernier scale.
AM.I.E.S7	Check the concentricity of a shaft.
AM.I.E.S8	Identify aircraft control cable components.
AM.I.E.S9	Fabricate a cable assembly using a swaged-end fitting.
AM.I.E.S10	Select the correct aluminum alloy for a structural repair.
AM.I.E.S11	Identify rivets by physical characteristics.
AM.I.E.S12	Determine suitability of materials for aircraft repairs.

| AM.I.E.S13 | Distinguish between heat-treated and non-heat-treated aluminum alloys. | |
| AM.I.E.S14 | Check for proper calibration of a micrometer. | |

I. General

Subject F. Ground Operations and Servicing

References	AC 20-35, AC 43.13-1, AC 150/5210-20; FAA-H-8083-30
Objective	The following knowledge, risk management, and skill elements are required for ground operations and servicing.
Knowledge	The applicant demonstrates understanding of:
AM.I.F.K1	Aircraft towing procedures.
AM.I.F.K2	Aircraft securing procedures.
AM.I.F.K3	Aviation fueling/defueling procedures.
AM.I.F.K4	Airport operation area procedures and ATC communications, including runway incursion prevention.
AM.I.F.K5	Engine starting, ground operation, and aircraft taxiing procedures.
AM.I.F.K6	Types/classes of fire extinguishers and procedures.
AM.I.F.K7	Aircraft oil, hydraulic and pneumatic, and deicing servicing procedures.
AM.I.F.K8	Oxygen system servicing procedures.
AM.I.F.K9	Characteristics of aviation gasoline and turbine fuels, including basic types and means of identification.
AM.I.F.K10	Fuel additives commonly used in the field.
AM.I.F.K11	Use of approved grades/types of fuel in aircraft engines.
AM.I.F.K12	Tool and hardware use and accountability.
AM.I.F.K13	Material handling.
AM.I.F.K14	Parts protections.
AM.I.F.K15	Hazardous materials, Safety Data Sheets (SDS), and PPE.
AM.I.F.K16	Foreign object damage effects.
Risk Management	The applicant demonstrates the ability to identify, assess, and mitigate risks associated with:
AM.I.F.R1	Preparing to tow an aircraft.
AM.I.F.R2	Connecting external power equipment to an aircraft.
AM.I.F.R3	Fueling/defueling ungrounded aircraft or using improper equipment.
AM.I.F.R4	Misfueling and using incorrect or contaminated fuel.
AM.I.F.R5	Oxygen system servicing.
AM.I.F.R6	Engine start/run-up without using a checklist.
AM.I.F.R7	Engine starting and ground operations.
AM.I.F.R8	Engine starting and operation while troubleshooting or adjusting engine controls.
AM.I.F.R9	Ground operation of an aircraft engine with cowling removed contrary to manufacturer instructions.
AM.I.F.R10	Ground operation of aircraft in the vicinity of other aircraft or ground support equipment.
Skills	The applicant demonstrates the ability to:
AM.I.F.S1	Perform a foreign object damage control procedure.
AM.I.F.S2	Connect external power to an aircraft.
AM.I.F.S3	Prepare an aircraft for towing.

AM.I.F.S4	Use appropriate hand signals for the movement of aircraft.
AM.I.F.S5	Inspect an aircraft fuel system for water and foreign object debris (FOD) contamination.
AM.I.F.S6	Identify different grades of aviation fuel.
AM.I.F.S7	Select an approved fuel for an aircraft.
AM.I.F.S8	Prepare an aircraft for fueling.
AM.I.F.S9	Follow a checklist to start up or shut down an aircraft reciprocating or turbine engine.
AM.I.F.S10	Identify procedures for extinguishing fires in an engine induction system.
AM.I.F.S11	Secure an aircraft.
AM.I.F.S12	Locate and explain procedures for securing a turbine-powered aircraft after engine shutdown.

Subject G. Cleaning and Corrosion Control

References	*AC 43.13-1; FAA-H-8083-30*
Objective	*The following knowledge, risk management, and skill elements are required for cleaning and corrosion control.*
Knowledge	*The applicant demonstrates understanding of:*
AM.I.G.K1	Aircraft cleaning procedures.
AM.I.G.K2	Corrosion theory and causation.
AM.I.G.K3	Types and effects of corrosion.
AM.I.G.K4	Corrosion-prone areas in aircraft.
AM.I.G.K5	Corrosion preventive maintenance procedures.
AM.I.G.K6	Corrosion identification and inspection.
AM.I.G.K7	Corrosion removal and treatment procedures.
AM.I.G.K8	Corrosion preventive compounds (CPC) (e.g., waxy sealants, thin-film dielectrics).
AM.I.G.K9	Selection of optimal CPC and frequency of treatment.
AM.I.G.K10	Use of high-pressure application equipment.
AM.I.G.K11	Improper use of cleaners on aluminum or composite materials.
AM.I.G.K12	Dissimilar metals causing accelerated corrosion and role of protective barriers to mitigate this risk.
AM.I.G.K13	Conversion coatings.
AM.I.G.K14	Materials used for protection of airframe structures.
AM.I.G.K15	Primer materials.
AM.I.G.K16	Topcoat materials.
AM.I.G.K17	Surface preparation for a desired finishing material.
AM.I.G.K18	Effects of ambient conditions on finishing materials.
AM.I.G.K19	Effects of improper surface preparation on finishing materials.
AM.I.G.K20	Regulatory requirements for replacing identification, registration markings, and placards.
AM.I.G.K21	Inspection of aircraft finishes.
AM.I.G.K22	Safety practices/precautions when using finishing materials (e.g., PPE, fire prevention).
AM.I.G.K23	Finishing materials application techniques and practices.
AM.I.G.K24	Control surface balance considerations after refinishing.
Risk Management	*The applicant demonstrates the ability to identify, assess, and mitigate risks associated with:*
AM.I.G.R1	Health concerns when using paints, solvents, finishing materials, and processes.
AM.I.G.R2	Ventilation.
AM.I.G.R3	Identification of materials and processes to be used for cleaning or corrosion treatment on a given part or structure to prevent further damage.
AM.I.G.R4	SDS PPE instructions for products during removal and treatment of corrosion.
AM.I.G.R5	Working with flammable chemicals.
AM.I.G.R6	Disposal of chemicals and waste materials.
AM.I.G.R7	Use of PPE when working with paints and solvents.
AM.I.G.R8	Application of finishing materials.

Skills	The applicant demonstrates the ability to:
AM.I.G.S1	Perform a portion of an aircraft corrosion inspection.
AM.I.G.S2	Identify, select, and use aircraft corrosion prevention/cleaning materials.
AM.I.G.S3	Apply corrosion prevention/coating materials.
AM.I.G.S4	Inspect finishes and identify defects.
AM.I.G.S5	Inspect an aircraft compartment for corrosion.
AM.I.G.S6	Identify procedures to clean and protect plastics.
AM.I.G.S7	Determine location and size requirements for aircraft registration numbers.
AM.I.G.S8	Prepare composite surface for painting.
AM.I.G.S9	Identify finishing materials and appropriate thinners.
AM.I.G.S10	Layout and mask a surface in preparation for painting.
AM.I.G.S11	Prepare metal surface for painting.
AM.I.G.S12	Determine what paint system can be used on a given aircraft.
AM.I.G.S13	Apply etch solution and conversion coating.
AM.I.G.S14	Identify types of protective finishes.

I. General

Subject H. Mathematics

References	*AC 43.13-1; FAA-H-8083-30*
Objective	*The following knowledge, risk management, and skill elements are required for mathematics as it relates to aircraft maintenance.*

Knowledge	*The applicant demonstrates understanding of:*
AM.I.H.K1	Areas of various geometrical shapes.
AM.I.H.K2	Volumes of various geometrical shapes.
AM.I.H.K3	Definitions, descriptions and use of geometrical terms, including but not limited to any of the following: polygon, pi, diameter, radius, and hypotenuse.
AM.I.H.K4	Ratio problems, including examples of where or how they may be used in relation to aircraft maintenance or system(s) operation.
AM.I.H.K5	Proportion and percentage problems, including examples of where or how they may be used in relation to aircraft maintenance or system(s) operation.
AM.I.H.K6	Algebraic operations, including examples of where or how they may be used in relation to aircraft maintenance.
AM.I.H.K7	Conditions or areas in which metric conversion may be necessary.
AM.I.H.K8	Scientific (exponential) notation, decimal notation, fractional notation, binary notation, and conversion between these various forms of numeric notation.
AM.I.H.K9	Rounding numbers.
AM.I.H.K10	Powers and special powers.
AM.I.H.K11	Measurement systems.
AM.I.H.K12	Use of positive and negative integers in mathematical operations.
AM.I.H.K13	Basic mathematic functions (addition, subtraction, multiplication, division).

Risk Management	*The applicant demonstrates the ability to identify, assess, and mitigate risks associated with:*
AM.I.H.R1	Precedence of operations when solving an algebraic equation.
AM.I.H.R2	Use of both positive and negative integers in mathematical operations.
AM.I.H.R3	Rounding off calculations.

Skills	*The applicant demonstrates the ability to:*
AM.I.H.S1	Determine the square root of given numbers.
AM.I.H.S2	Compute the volume of a cylinder.
AM.I.H.S3	Compute the area of a wing.
AM.I.H.S4	Calculate the volume of a shape, such as a baggage compartment or fuel tank.
AM.I.H.S5	Convert between fractional and decimal numbers.
AM.I.H.S6	Compare two numerical values using ratios.
AM.I.H.S7	Compute compression ratio.
AM.I.H.S8	Compute the torque value when converting from inch-pounds to foot-pounds or from foot-pounds to inch-pounds.

Subject I. Regulations, Maintenance Forms, Records, and Publications

References	*14 CFR; AC 43.13-1, AC 43-9; FAA-H-8083-30*
Objective	*The following knowledge, risk management, and skill elements are required for regulations, maintenance forms, records, and publications.*
Knowledge	*The applicant demonstrates understanding of:*
AM.I.I.K1	Privileges and limitations of a mechanic certificate.
AM.I.I.K2	Recent experience requirements and how to re-establish once lost.
AM.I.I.K3	Maintenance record entry for approval for return to service after maintenance and alterations.
AM.I.I.K4	Maintenance record entry for approval for return to service after inspection.
AM.I.I.K5	The purpose and use of FAA forms (e.g., FAA Forms 337, 8010-4, 8100-2, 8130-3).
AM.I.I.K6	Maintenance terminology as defined in 14 CFR part 1 (e.g., time in service, maintenance, preventive maintenance, major alteration, major repair, minor alteration, minor repair).
AM.I.I.K7	Criteria and responsibility for determining whether a repair or alteration is major or minor.
AM.I.I.K8	The regulatory framework, including general subject matter of the parts of 14 CFR relevant to aircraft maintenance and mechanics.
AM.I.I.K9	Agency publications and guidance materials, including aircraft specifications, TCDSs, advisory circulars (AC), and airworthiness directives (AD).
AM.I.I.K10	Alternative Method of Compliance (AMOC) for an AD.
AM.I.I.K11	Manufacturer publications, including maintenance manuals, service bulletins, maintenance alerts, and master minimum equipment lists.
AM.I.I.K12	FAA databases and resources available, including TCDSs and supplemental type certificates.
AM.I.I.K13	Compliance requirements for manufacturer-specified methods, techniques, and practices.
AM.I.I.K14	Compliance requirements for manufacturer-specified maintenance and inspection intervals.
AM.I.I.K15	FAA-approved maintenance data, including maintenance manuals and other methods, techniques, and practices acceptable by the administrator.
AM.I.I.K16	Difference between approved data and acceptable data, and when each is required.
AM.I.I.K17	FAA-approved airworthiness limitations.
AM.I.I.K18	Alert, caution, and warning indications; and the basic definition of warnings, cautions, and notes that are used in maintenance and operating manuals.
AM.I.I.K19	Inoperative equipment.
AM.I.I.K20	Discrepancy records or placards.
AM.I.I.K21	Usable on (effectivity) codes in parts manuals.
AM.I.I.K22	Methods used to establish the serial number effectivity of an item.
AM.I.I.K23	Mechanic address change notification procedures.
Risk Management	*The applicant demonstrates the ability to identify, assess, and mitigate risks associated with:*
AM.I.I.R1	Completeness or accuracy of documentation.
AM.I.I.R2	Use of SDS.
AM.I.I.R3	Complacency during documentation phase of maintenance procedures.
AM.I.I.R4	Adherence to warnings, cautions, or notes in maintenance and operational manuals.
AM.I.I.R5	Determination of component applicability to a given aircraft.

Skills	The applicant demonstrates the ability to:
AM.I.I.S1	Complete an FAA Form 337 for a major repair or alteration.
AM.I.I.S2	Examine an FAA Form 337 for accuracy.
AM.I.I.S3	Determine an aircraft's inspection status by reviewing the aircraft's maintenance records.
AM.I.I.S4	Complete an aircraft maintenance record entry for the compliance of a reoccurring AD for a specific airframe, aircraft engine, appliance, or propeller.
AM.I.I.S5	Compare an equipment list for an aircraft to equipment installed.
AM.I.I.S6	Locate applicable FAA aircraft specifications and FAA TCDS for an aircraft or component.
AM.I.I.S7	Complete an aircraft maintenance record entry for return to service.
AM.I.I.S8	Determine applicability of an AD.
AM.I.I.S9	Check a Technical Standard Order (TSO) or part manufacturing authorization for the proper markings.
AM.I.I.S10	Use a manufacturer's illustrated parts catalog to locate a specific part number and applicability.
AM.I.I.S11	Locate supplemental type certificates applicable to a specific aircraft.
AM.I.I.S12	Determine the conformity of aircraft instrument range markings and placarding.
AM.I.I.S13	Determine approved replacement parts for installation on a given aircraft.
AM.I.I.S14	Determine maximum allowable weight of a specific aircraft.
AM.I.I.S15	Determine whether a given repair or alteration is major or minor.
AM.I.I.S16	Determine applicability of approved data for a major repair.
AM.I.I.S17	Explain the difference between "approved data" (required for major repair/alteration) and "acceptable data" (required for minor repair/alteration).
AM.I.I.S18	Complete a 100-hour inspection aircraft maintenance record entry.

I. General

Subject J. Physics for Aviation

References	*AC 43.13-1; FAA-H-8083-30*
Objective	*The following knowledge, risk management, and skill elements are required for aviation physics.*
Knowledge	*The applicant demonstrates understanding of:*
AM.I.J.K1	Matter and energy.
AM.I.J.K2	Work, power, force, and motion.
AM.I.J.K3	Simple machines and mechanics.
AM.I.J.K4	Heat and pressure.
AM.I.J.K5	Bernoulli's Principle.
AM.I.J.K6	Newton's Law of Motion.
AM.I.J.K7	Gas law and fluid mechanics.
AM.I.J.K8	Theory of flight (aerodynamics).
AM.I.J.K9	Standard atmosphere and factors affecting atmospheric conditions.
AM.I.J.K10	Primary and secondary aircraft flight controls.
AM.I.J.K11	Additional aerodynamic devices, including vortex generators, wing fences, and stall strips.
AM.I.J.K12	Relationship between temperature, density, weight, and volume.
AM.I.J.K13	Force, area, or pressure in a specific application.
Risk Management	*The applicant demonstrates the ability to identify, assess, and mitigate risks associated with:*
AM.I.J.R1	Changes in aircraft and engine performance due to density altitude.
AM.I.J.R2	Effect a repair can have on a flight surface.
AM.I.J.R3	Use of performance/testing data.
AM.I.J.R4	Use of related units of measure (e.g., Celsius vs. Fahrenheit).
Skills	*The applicant demonstrates the ability to:*
AM.I.J.S1	Convert temperature units (e.g., from Celsius to Fahrenheit).
AM.I.J.S2	Determine density altitude.
AM.I.J.S3	Determine pressure altitude.
AM.I.J.S4	Calculate force, area, or pressure in a specific application.
AM.I.J.S5	Demonstrate the mechanical advantage of various types of levers.
AM.I.J.S6	Design an inclined plane on paper, indicating the mechanical advantage.
AM.I.J.S7	Identify changes in pressure and velocity as a fluid passes through a venturi.
AM.I.J.S8	Calculate horsepower.

I. General

Subject K. Inspection Concepts and Techniques

References	*AC 43.13-1; FAA-H-8083-30*
Objective	*The following knowledge, risk management, and skill elements are required for aircraft inspection concepts and techniques.*
Knowledge	*The applicant demonstrates understanding of:*
AM.I.K.K1	Measuring tools, including calipers, micrometers, and gauges.
AM.I.K.K2	Calibration and tool accuracy requirements.
AM.I.K.K3	Nondestructive Testing (NDT) procedures and methods.
AM.I.K.K4	Aircraft inspection programs (e.g., progressive, 100-hour, annual, and other FAA-approved inspections).
AM.I.K.K5	Aircraft inspection methods and tools for materials, hardware, and processes.
Risk Management	*The applicant demonstrates the ability to identify, assess, and mitigate risks associated with:*
AM.I.K.R1	Demagnetizing a component following a magnetic particle inspection.
AM.I.K.R2	Using precision measuring instruments.
AM.I.K.R3	Calibration of precision measuring equipment.
AM.I.K.R4	Selection of inspection techniques.
AM.I.K.R5	Damage prevention to aircraft components and test equipment when using an ohmmeter.
Skills	*The applicant demonstrates the ability to:*
AM.I.K.S1	Use Vernier calipers.
AM.I.K.S2	Use micrometers.
AM.I.K.S3	Use measurement gauges.
AM.I.K.S4	Perform a visual inspection.
AM.I.K.S5	Perform a dye penetrant inspection.
AM.I.K.S6	Inspect aircraft for compliance with an AD.
AM.I.K.S7	Identify NDT methods for composite, surface metal, and subsurface metal defects.
AM.I.K.S8	Perform a tap test on a composite component.

I. General

Subject L. Human Factors

References	*AC 43.13-1; FAA-H-8083-30*
Objective	*The following knowledge, risk management, and skill elements are required for human factors.*
Knowledge	*The applicant demonstrates understanding of:*
AM.I.L.K1	Safety culture and organizational factors.
AM.I.L.K2	Human error principles.
AM.I.L.K3	Event investigation.
AM.I.L.K4	Human performance and limitations.
AM.I.L.K5	Physical and social environment.
AM.I.L.K6	Communication/reporting of hazards.
AM.I.L.K7	Teamwork and leadership.
AM.I.L.K8	Professionalism and integrity.
AM.I.L.K9	Shift and task turnover.
AM.I.L.K10	Conditions/preconditions for unsafe acts.
AM.I.L.K11	Types of human errors.
Risk Management	*The applicant demonstrates the ability to identify, assess, and mitigate risks associated with:*
AM.I.L.R1	Selective reporting of hazards.
AM.I.L.R2	Fatigue management and fitness for duty.
AM.I.L.R3	Non-invasive, condition-monitoring technologies.
Skills	*The applicant demonstrates the ability to:*
AM.I.L.S1	File a Malfunction or Defect Report.
AM.I.L.S2	Brief a shift turnover for continuity of work.
AM.I.L.S3	Locate information regarding human factors errors.

II. Airframe
Subject A. Metallic Structures

References	*AC 43.13-1; FAA-H-8083-31*
Objective	*The following knowledge, risk management, and skill elements are required for aircraft metallic structures.*
Knowledge	*The applicant demonstrates understanding of:*
AM.II.A.K1	Inspection/testing of metal structures.
AM.II.A.K2	Types of sheet metal defects.
AM.II.A.K3	Selection of sheet metal repair materials.
AM.II.A.K4	Layout, forming, and drilling of sheet metal components.
AM.II.A.K5	Selection of rivets, hardware, and fasteners for a sheet metal repair.
AM.II.A.K6	Heat treatment processes for aluminum.
AM.II.A.K7	Rivet layout.
AM.II.A.K8	Rivet removal and installation methods.
AM.II.A.K9	Maintenance safety practices/precautions for sheet metal repairs or fabrications.
AM.II.A.K10	Flame welding gases.
AM.II.A.K11	Storage/handling of welding gases.
AM.II.A.K12	Flame welding practices and techniques.
AM.II.A.K13	Inert-gas welding practices and techniques.
AM.II.A.K14	Purpose and types of shielding gases.
AM.II.A.K15	Types of steel tubing welding repairs.
AM.II.A.K16	Procedures for weld repairs.
AM.II.A.K17	Types of structures and their characteristics.
Risk Management	*The applicant demonstrates the ability to identify, assess, and mitigate risks associated with:*
AM.II.A.R1	Selection of repair materials.
AM.II.A.R2	Utilizing maintenance safety practices/precautions for sheet metal structures.
AM.II.A.R3	Use of PPE when working with sheet metal structures.
AM.II.A.R4	Handling, storage, and use of compressed gas bottles.
AM.II.A.R5	Use of electric welding equipment.
Skills	*The applicant demonstrates the ability to:*
AM.II.A.S1	Install and remove solid rivets.
AM.II.A.S2	Install and remove a blind rivet.
AM.II.A.S3	Determine applicability of sheet metal for a repair in a specific application.
AM.II.A.S4	Select and install special purpose fasteners.
AM.II.A.S5	Design a repair using a manufacturer's structural repair manual.
AM.II.A.S6	Prepare and install a patch to repair an aircraft or component.
AM.II.A.S7	Make a drawing of a repair, including the number of rivets and size of sheet metal required.
AM.II.A.S8	Remove a repair that was installed with rivets.
AM.II.A.S9	Trim and form a piece of sheet metal to fit a prepared area.
AM.II.A.S10	Fabricate an aluminum part in accordance with a drawing.

AM.II.A.S11	Determine a rivet pattern for a specific repair.	
AM.II.A.S12	Countersink rivet holes in sheet metal.	47
AM.II.A.S13	Perform a repair on a damaged aluminum sheet.	
AM.II.A.S14	Determine extent of damage and decide if metallic structure is repairable.	

II. Airframe
Subject B. Non-Metallic Structures

References	*AC 43.13-1; FAA-H-8083-31*
Objective	*The following knowledge, risk management, and skill elements are required for aircraft non-metallic structures.*

Knowledge	*The applicant demonstrates understanding of:*
AM.II.B.K1	Wood structures, including inspection techniques, tools, and practices for wood structures.
AM.II.B.K2	Effects of moisture/humidity on wood and fabric coverings.
AM.II.B.K3	Types and general characteristics of wood used in aircraft structures.
AM.II.B.K4	Permissible substitutes and other materials used in the construction and repair of wood structures.
AM.II.B.K5	Acceptable and unacceptable wood defects.
AM.II.B.K6	Wood repair techniques and practices.
AM.II.B.K7	Factors used in determining the proper type covering material.
AM.II.B.K8	Types of approved aircraft covering material.
AM.II.B.K9	Seams commonly used with aircraft covering.
AM.II.B.K10	Covering textile terms.
AM.II.B.K11	Structure surface preparation.
AM.II.B.K12	Covering methods commonly used.
AM.II.B.K13	Covering means of attachment.
AM.II.B.K14	Areas on aircraft covering most susceptible to deterioration.
AM.II.B.K15	Aircraft covering preservation/restoration.
AM.II.B.K16	Inspection of aircraft covering.
AM.II.B.K17	Covering repair techniques and practices.
AM.II.B.K18	Inspection/testing of composite structures.
AM.II.B.K19	Types of composite structure defects.
AM.II.B.K20	Composite structure fiber, core, and matrix materials.
AM.II.B.K21	Composite materials storage practices and shelf life.
AM.II.B.K22	Composite repair methods, techniques, fasteners, and practices.
AM.II.B.K23	Thermoplastic material inspection/types of defects.
AM.II.B.K24	Thermoplastic material storage and handling.
AM.II.B.K25	Thermoplastic material installation procedures.
AM.II.B.K26	Care and maintenance of windows.
AM.II.B.K27	Window temporary and permanent repairs.
AM.II.B.K28	Maintenance safety practices/precautions for composite materials/structures, and windows.
AM.II.B.K29	Inspecting restraints and upholstery.

Risk Management	*The applicant demonstrates the ability to identify, assess, and mitigate risks associated with:*
AM.II.B.R1	Selection of glue (adhesive) or fasteners for aircraft structure.
AM.II.B.R2	Composite structure repairs.
AM.II.B.R3	Exposure to materials used in composite repair.

AM.II.B.R4	Storage of composite materials.	
AM.II.B.R5	Measuring and mixing of materials associated with composite construction.	
AM.II.B.R6	Use of materials that are not part of an approved repair system.	
AM.II.B.R7	Material shelf-life.	
Skills	*The applicant demonstrates the ability to:*	
AM.II.B.S1	Identify appropriate fasteners on composite structures.	
AM.II.B.S2	Inspect and repair fiberglass.	
AM.II.B.S3	Inspect composite, plastic, or glass-laminated structures.	
AM.II.B.S4	Clean and inspect acrylic type windshields.	
AM.II.B.S5	Locate and explain procedures for a temporary repair to a side window.	
AM.II.B.S6	Locate and explain the procedures for tying a modified seine knot.	
AM.II.B.S7	Prepare composite surface for painting.	
AM.II.B.S8	Perform a tap test on composite material.	
AM.II.B.S9	Locate and explain repair standard dimensions.	
AM.II.B.S10	Locate and explain repair procedures for elongated bolt holes.	
AM.II.B.S11	Determine extent of damage and decide if nonmetallic structure is repairable.	
AM.II.B.S12	Perform lay up for a repair to a composite panel, including preparation for vacuum bagging, using a manufacturer's repair manual.	

II. Airframe
Subject C. Flight Controls

References	*AC 43.13-1; FAA-H-8083-31*
Objective	*The following knowledge, risk management, and skill elements are required for aircraft flight controls.*
Knowledge	*The applicant demonstrates understanding of:*
AM.II.C.K1	Control cables.
AM.II.C.K2	Control cable maintenance.
AM.II.C.K3	Cable connectors.
AM.II.C.K4	Cable guides.
AM.II.C.K5	Control stops.
AM.II.C.K6	Push-pull tubes.
AM.II.C.K7	Torque tubes.
AM.II.C.K8	Bellcranks.
AM.II.C.K9	Flutter and flight control balance.
AM.II.C.K10	Rigging of aircraft flight controls.
AM.II.C.K11	Aircraft flight controls and stabilizer systems.
AM.II.C.K12	Other aerodynamic wing features.
AM.II.C.K13	Secondary and auxiliary control surfaces.
Risk Management	*The applicant demonstrates the ability to identify, assess, and mitigate risks associated with:*
AM.II.C.R1	Use of and interpretation of a cable tension chart.
AM.II.C.R2	Rigging aircraft flight controls.
AM.II.C.R3	Selection and use of lifting equipment used to move aircraft components into place for assembly.
AM.II.C.R4	Maintaining a calibration schedule for cable tension meters and other rigging equipment.
AM.II.C.R5	Use and interpretation of cable tensiometers.
Skills	*The applicant demonstrates the ability to:*
AM.II.C.S1	Identify fixed-wing aircraft rigging adjustment locations.
AM.II.C.S2	Identify control surfaces that provide movement about an aircraft's axes.
AM.II.C.S3	Inspect a primary and secondary flight control surface.
AM.II.C.S4	Remove and reinstall a primary flight control surface.
AM.II.C.S5	Inspect primary control cables.
AM.II.C.S6	Adjust and secure a primary flight control cable.
AM.II.C.S7	Adjust push-pull flight control systems.
AM.II.C.S8	Check the balance of a flight control surface.
AM.II.C.S9	Determine allowable axial play limits for a flight control bearing.
AM.II.C.S10	Inspect a trim tab for freeplay, travel, and operation.
AM.II.C.S11	Balance a control surface.
AM.II.C.S12	Fabricate a primary flight control cable.
AM.II.C.S13	Locate aircraft flight control travel limits.

II. Airframe

Subject D. Airframe Inspection

References	*AC 43.13-1; FAA-H-8083-31*
Objective	*The following knowledge, risk management, and skill elements are required for airframe inspections.*
Knowledge	*The applicant demonstrates understanding of:*
AM.II.D.K1	Inspection requirements under 14 CFR part 91.
AM.II.D.K2	Maintenance recordkeeping requirements under 14 CFR part 43.
AM.II.D.K3	Requirements for complying with ADs.
AM.II.D.K4	Identification of life-limited parts and their replacement interval.
AM.II.D.K5	Special inspections.
AM.II.D.K6	Use of FAA-approved data.
AM.II.D.K7	Compliance with service letters, service bulletins, instructions for continued airworthiness, or ADs.
AM.II.D.K8	CFRs applicable to inspection and airworthiness.
AM.II.D.K9	Corrosion types and identification.
Risk Management	*The applicant demonstrates the ability to identify, assess, and mitigate risks associated with:*
AM.II.D.R1	Interpretation of inspection instructions, which can lead to over or under maintenance being performed.
AM.II.D.R2	Visual inspection and where to apply it.
AM.II.D.R3	Performing radiographic inspections.
AM.II.D.R4	Selection and use of checklists and other maintenance publications.
AM.II.D.R5	Maintenance record documentation.
Skills	*The applicant demonstrates the ability to:*
AM.II.D.S1	Perform an airframe inspection, including a records check.
AM.II.D.S2	Perform a portion of a 100-hour inspection in accordance with 14 CFR part 43.
AM.II.D.S3	Enter results of a 100-hour inspection in a maintenance record.
AM.II.D.S4	Determine compliance with a specific AD.
AM.II.D.S5	Provide a checklist for conducting a 100-hour inspection.
AM.II.D.S6	Determine if any additional inspections are required during a particular 100-hour inspection; (i.e., 300-hour filter replacement).
AM.II.D.S7	Inspect seat and seatbelt, including TSO markings.

II. Airframe

Subject E. Landing Gear Systems

References	*AC 43.13-1; FAA-H-8083-31*
Objective	*The following knowledge, risk management, and skill elements are required for aircraft landing gear systems.*
Knowledge	*The applicant demonstrates understanding of:*
AM.II.E.K1	Fixed and retractable landing gear systems.
AM.II.E.K2	Fixed and retractable landing gear components.
AM.II.E.K3	Landing gear strut servicing/lubrication.
AM.II.E.K4	Inspection of bungee and spring steel landing gear systems.
AM.II.E.K5	Steering systems.
AM.II.E.K6	Landing gear position and warning system inspection, check, and servicing.
AM.II.E.K7	Brake assembly servicing and inspection.
AM.II.E.K8	Anti-skid system components and operation.
AM.II.E.K9	Wheel, brake, and tire construction.
AM.II.E.K10	Tire storage, care, and servicing.
AM.II.E.K11	Landing gear and tire and wheel safety and inspection.
AM.II.E.K12	Brake actuating systems.
AM.II.E.K13	Alternative landing gear systems (e.g., skis, floats).
Risk Management	*The applicant demonstrates the ability to identify, assess, and mitigate risks associated with:*
AM.II.E.R1	Landing gear and tire and wheel practices/precautions.
AM.II.E.R2	Use of aircraft jacks.
AM.II.E.R3	High pressure fluids and gases.
AM.II.E.R4	Storage and handling of hydraulic fluids.
AM.II.E.R5	High pressure strut or system disassembly.
AM.II.E.R6	Operation of retractable landing gear systems around personnel.
Skills	*The applicant demonstrates the ability to:*
AM.II.E.S1	Inspect and service landing gear.
AM.II.E.S2	Inspect, check, and service an anti-skid system.
AM.II.E.S3	Locate and explain procedures for checking operation of an anti-skid warning system.
AM.II.E.S4	Locate and explain troubleshooting procedures for an anti-skid system.
AM.II.E.S5	Jack aircraft.
AM.II.E.S6	Troubleshoot a landing gear retraction check.
AM.II.E.S7	Inspect wheels, brakes, bearings, and tires.
AM.II.E.S8	Remove and replace brake lining(s).
AM.II.E.S9	Service landing gear air/oil shock strut.
AM.II.E.S10	Bleed air from a hydraulic brake system.
AM.II.E.S11	Troubleshoot hydraulic brake systems.
AM.II.E.S12	Remove, inspect, and install a wheel brake assembly.
AM.II.E.S13	Inspect a tire for defects.

AM.II.E.S14	Locate tire storage practices.
AM.II.E.S15	Replace air/oil shock strut air valve.
AM.II.E.S16	Troubleshoot an air/oil shock strut.
AM.II.E.S17	Service a nose-wheel shimmy damper.
AM.II.E.S18	Inspect nose-wheel steering system for proper adjustment.
AM.II.E.S19	Locate and explain the process for checking landing gear alignment.
AM.II.E.S20	Replace master brake cylinder packing seals.
AM.II.E.S21	Troubleshoot aircraft steering system.
AM.II.E.S22	Identify landing gear position and warning system components.
AM.II.E.S23	Troubleshoot landing gear position and warning systems.
AM.II.E.S24	Inspect and repair landing gear position indicating system.
AM.II.E.S25	Adjust the operation of a landing gear warning system.
AM.II.E.S26	Remove, install, and adjust a landing gear down-lock switch.
AM.II.E.S27	Inspect a brake for serviceability.
AM.II.E.S28	Troubleshoot nose-wheel shimmy.
AM.II.E.S29	Inspect tube landing gear for damage.

II. Airframe

Subject F. Hydraulic and Pneumatic Systems

References	AC 43.13-1; FAA-H-8083-31
Objective	The following knowledge, risk management, and skill elements are required for aircraft hydraulic and pneumatic systems.
Knowledge	The applicant demonstrates understanding of:
AM.II.F.K1	Hydraulic system components and fluids.
AM.II.F.K2	Hydraulic system operation.
AM.II.F.K3	Hydraulic system servicing requirements.
AM.II.F.K4	Hydraulic system inspection, check, servicing, and troubleshooting.
AM.II.F.K5	Pneumatic system types and components.
AM.II.F.K6	Pneumatic system servicing requirements.
AM.II.F.K7	Servicing, function, and operation of accumulators.
AM.II.F.K8	Types of hydraulic/pneumatic seals and fluid/seal compatibility.
AM.II.F.K9	Hoses, lines, and fittings.
AM.II.F.K10	Pressure regulators, restrictors, and valves.
AM.II.F.K11	Filter maintenance procedures.
Risk Management	The applicant demonstrates the ability to identify, assess, and mitigate risks associated with:
AM.II.F.R1	Relieving system pressure prior to system servicing or disassembly.
AM.II.F.R2	High pressure gases and fluids.
AM.II.F.R3	Storage and handling of hydraulic fluids.
AM.II.F.R4	Cross-contamination of hydraulic fluids.
AM.II.F.R5	Compatibility between hydraulic seals and hydraulic fluids.
Skills	The applicant demonstrates the ability to:
AM.II.F.S1	Identify different types of hydraulic fluids.
AM.II.F.S2	Identify different packing seals.
AM.II.F.S3	Install seals and backup rings in a hydraulic component.
AM.II.F.S4	Remove and install a selector valve.
AM.II.F.S5	Check a pressure regulator and adjust as necessary.
AM.II.F.S6	Remove, clean, inspect, and install a hydraulic system filter.
AM.II.F.S7	Service a hydraulic system accumulator.
AM.II.F.S8	Service a hydraulic system reservoir.
AM.II.F.S9	Remove, install, and perform an operational check of a hydraulic pump.
AM.II.F.S10	Locate procedures for checking pneumatic/bleed air overheat warning systems.
AM.II.F.S11	Purge air from a hydraulic system.
AM.II.F.S12	Remove and install a system pressure relief valve.
AM.II.F.S13	Inspect a hydraulic or pneumatic system for leaks.
AM.II.F.S14	Troubleshoot a hydraulic or pneumatic system for leaks.
AM.II.F.S15	Locate and explain hydraulic fluid servicing instructions and identify/select fluid for a given aircraft.
AM.II.F.S16	Locate installation procedures for a seal, backup ring, or gasket.

II. Airframe

Subject G. Environmental Systems

References	*AC 43.13-1; FAA-H-8083-31*
Objective	*The following knowledge, risk management, and skill elements are required for aircraft environmental systems.*

Knowledge	*The applicant demonstrates understanding of:*
AM.II.G.K1	Pressurization systems.
AM.II.G.K2	Bleed air heating.
AM.II.G.K3	Aircraft instrument cooling.
AM.II.G.K4	Exhaust heat exchanger and system component(s) function, operation, and inspection procedures.
AM.II.G.K5	Combustion heater and system component(s) function, operation, and inspection procedures.
AM.II.G.K6	Vapor-cycle system and system component(s) operation, servicing, and inspection procedures.
AM.II.G.K7	Air-cycle system and system component(s) operation and inspection procedures.
AM.II.G.K8	Cabin pressurization and system component(s) operation and inspection procedures.
AM.II.G.K9	Types of oxygen systems and oxygen system component(s) operation (e.g., chemical generator, pressure cylinder).
AM.II.G.K10	Oxygen system maintenance and inspection procedures.

Risk Management	*The applicant demonstrates the ability to identify, assess, and mitigate risks associated with:*
AM.II.G.R1	Oxygen system maintenance.
AM.II.G.R2	Recovery of vapor-cycle refrigerant.
AM.II.G.R3	Handling or performing maintenance on, chemical oxygen generating systems.
AM.II.G.R4	Storage, handling, and use of compressed gas cylinder and high pressure systems.
AM.II.G.R5	Manufacturer's recommended servicing procedures, including refrigerant types.
AM.II.G.R6	Maintenance of combustion heaters.

Skills	*The applicant demonstrates the ability to:*
AM.II.G.S1	Inspect an oxygen system.
AM.II.G.S2	Purge an oxygen system prior to servicing.
AM.II.G.S3	Service an oxygen system.
AM.II.G.S4	Clean and inspect a pilot emergency oxygen mask and supply hoses.
AM.II.G.S5	Inspect an oxygen system pressure regulator.
AM.II.G.S6	Inspect an oxygen system cylinder for serviceability.
AM.II.G.S7	Inspect a chemical oxygen generator for serviceability and safe handling.
AM.II.G.S8	Locate the procedures to troubleshoot a combustion heater.
AM.II.G.S9	Locate the procedures for servicing a refrigerant (vapor-cycle) system.
AM.II.G.S10	Inspect a combustion heater fuel system for leaks.
AM.II.G.S11	Locate the troubleshooting procedures for an air-cycle system.
AM.II.G.S12	Troubleshoot an air-cycle air conditioning system.
AM.II.G.S13	Inspect a cabin heater system equipped with an exhaust heat exchanger for cracks.
AM.II.G.S14	Clean and inspect an outflow valve for a pressurization system.
AM.II.G.S15	Locate troubleshooting procedures for a pressurization system.

II. Airframe

Subject H. Aircraft Instrument Systems

References	*14 CFR parts 43, 91; AC 25-11, AC 43.13-1, AC 43-215; FAA-H-8083-31*
Objective	*The following knowledge, risk management, and skill elements are required for aircraft instrument systems.*
Knowledge	*The applicant demonstrates understanding of:*
AM.II.H.K1	Annunciator indicating systems and the meaning of warning, caution, and advisory lights.
AM.II.H.K2	Magnetic compass inspection and operation.
AM.II.H.K3	Magnetic compass swinging procedures.
AM.II.H.K4	Pressure indicating instruments.
AM.II.H.K5	Temperature indicating instruments.
AM.II.H.K6	Position indication sensors and instruments.
AM.II.H.K7	Gyroscopic instruments.
AM.II.H.K8	Direction indicating instruments.
AM.II.H.K9	Instrument vacuum and pneumatic systems.
AM.II.H.K10	Pitot-static system.
AM.II.H.K11	Fuel quantity indicating systems.
AM.II.H.K12	Instrument range markings.
AM.II.H.K13	Electronic displays.
AM.II.H.K14	Electrostatic sensitive devices.
AM.II.H.K15	Built-in test equipment.
AM.II.H.K16	Electronic flight instrument system.
AM.II.H.K17	Engine indication and crew alerting system.
AM.II.H.K18	Head-up displays (HUDs).
AM.II.H.K19	14 CFR parts 43 and 91 requirements for static system leak checks.
AM.II.H.K20	Instrument limitations, conditions, and characteristics.
AM.II.H.K21	Angle of attack and stall warning systems.
AM.II.H.K22	Takeoff and landing gear configuration warning systems.
AM.II.H.K23	Aircraft bonding and protection.
AM.II.H.K24	Instrument or instrument panel removal and installation.
Risk Management	*The applicant demonstrates the ability to identify, assess, and mitigate risks associated with:*
AM.II.H.R1	Use of pressurized air and water during maintenance or cleaning of aircraft instrument systems.
AM.II.H.R2	Actions in response to a reported intermittent warning or caution annunciator light illumination.
AM.II.H.R3	Performing maintenance on equipment identified as electrostatic-sensitive.
AM.II.H.R4	Handling of mechanical gyros or instruments containing mechanical gyros.
AM.II.H.R5	Performing a pitot/static system test.
Skills	*The applicant demonstrates the ability to:*
AM.II.H.S1	Perform a static system leak test.
AM.II.H.S2	Remove and install an instrument.
AM.II.H.S3	Install range marks on an instrument glass.

AM.II.H.S4	Determine barometric pressure using an altimeter.	
AM.II.H.S5	Check for proper range markings on an instrument.	
AM.II.H.S6	Inspect a magnetic compass.	
AM.II.H.S7	Locate the procedures for troubleshooting a vacuum-operated instrument system.	
AM.II.H.S8	Select proper altimeter for installation on a given aircraft.	
AM.II.H.S9	Identify exhaust gas temperature system components.	
AM.II.H.S10	Inspect a vacuum system filter for serviceability.	
AM.II.H.S11	Adjust gyro/instrument air pressure/vacuum.	
AM.II.H.S12	Inspect an aircraft's alternate air (static) source.	
AM.II.H.S13	Locate and explain the adjustment procedures for a stall warning system.	
AM.II.H.S14	Inspect outside air temperature gauge for condition and operation.	

II. Airframe

Subject I. Communication and Navigation Systems

References	*14 CFR part 91; AC 43.13-1, AC 43.13-2; FAA-H-8083-31*
Objective	*The following knowledge, risk management, and skill elements are required for aircraft communication and navigation systems.*
Knowledge	*The applicant demonstrates understanding of:*
AM.II.I.K1	Radio operating principles.
AM.II.I.K2	Radio components.
AM.II.I.K3	Antenna, static discharge wicks, and avionics identification, inspection, and mounting requirements.
AM.II.I.K4	Interphone and intercom systems.
AM.II.I.K5	Very high frequency (VHF), high frequency (HF), and SATCOM systems.
AM.II.I.K6	Aircraft Communication Addressing and Reporting System (ACARS) theory, components, and operation.
AM.II.I.K7	Emergency locator transmitter (ELT).
AM.II.I.K8	Automatic direction finder (ADF).
AM.II.I.K9	VHF omnidirectional range (VOR) theory, components, and operation.
AM.II.I.K10	Distance measuring equipment (DME) theory, components, and operation.
AM.II.I.K11	Instrument landing system (ILS) theory, components, and operation.
AM.II.I.K12	Global positioning system (GPS) theory, components, and operation.
AM.II.I.K13	Traffic collision avoidance system (TCAS), theory, components, and operation.
AM.II.I.K14	Weather radar.
AM.II.I.K15	Ground proximity warning system (GPWS) theory, components, and operation.
AM.II.I.K16	Autopilot theory, components, and operation.
AM.II.I.K17	Auto-throttle theory, components, and operation.
AM.II.I.K18	Stability augmentation systems (SAS) (Rotorcraft).
AM.II.I.K19	Radio altimeter (RA) theory, components, and operation.
AM.II.I.K20	Automatic Dependent Surveillance-Broadcast (ADS-B) theory, components, and operation.
AM.II.I.K21	Transponder/encoder system.
Risk Management	*The applicant demonstrates the ability to identify, assess, and mitigate risks associated with:*
AM.II.I.R1	ELT testing procedures.
AM.II.I.R2	Performing maintenance on high power/high frequency systems (e.g., weather radar and SATCOM).
AM.II.I.R3	Wire harness routing.
AM.II.I.R4	Mounting antennas.
AM.II.I.R5	Electro-static discharge.
AM.II.I.R6	Working around live electrical systems.
Skills	*The applicant demonstrates the ability to:*
AM.II.I.S1	Make a list of required placards for communication and navigation avionic equipment.
AM.II.I.S2	Locate and explain autopilot inspection procedures.

AM.II.I.S3	List autopilot major components.
AM.II.I.S4	Locate and identify navigation and communication antennas.
AM.II.I.S5	Check VHF communications for operation.
AM.II.I.S6	Inspect a coaxial cable installation for security.
AM.II.I.S7	Check an emergency locator transmitter for operation.
AM.II.I.S8	Inspect ELT batteries for expiration date and locate proper testing procedures.
AM.II.I.S9	Inspect electronic equipment mounting base for security and condition.
AM.II.I.S10	Inspect electronic equipment shock mount bonding jumpers for resistance.
AM.II.I.S11	Inspect static discharge wicks for security and resistance.
AM.II.I.S12	Inspect a radio installation for security.
AM.II.I.S13	Locate and explain the installation procedures for antennas, including mounting and coaxial connections.

II. Airframe

Subject J. Aircraft Fuel Systems

References	*AC 43.13-1; FAA-H-8083-31*
Objective	*The following knowledge, risk management, and skill elements are required for aircraft fuel systems.*
Knowledge	*The applicant demonstrates understanding of:*
AM.II.J.K1	Fuel system types.
AM.II.J.K2	Fuel system components, including filters and selector valves.
AM.II.J.K3	Aircraft fuel tanks/cells
AM.II.J.K4	Fuel flow.
AM.II.J.K5	Fuel transfer, fueling, and defueling.
AM.II.J.K6	Fuel jettisoning/dump systems.
AM.II.J.K7	Characteristics of fuel types.
AM.II.J.K8	Fuel system maintenance and inspection.
AM.II.J.K9	Fuel quantity indication.
Risk Management	*The applicant demonstrates the ability to identify, assess, and mitigate risks associated with:*
AM.II.J.R1	Fuel system maintenance.
AM.II.J.R2	Fuel system contamination.
AM.II.J.R3	Fuel spills.
AM.II.J.R4	Fuel system maintenance requiring fuel tank entry.
AM.II.J.R5	Defueling aircraft.
Skills	*The applicant demonstrates the ability to:*
AM.II.J.S1	Inspect, check, troubleshoot, or repair a fuel system.
AM.II.J.S2	Inspect a metal, bladder, or integral fuel tank.
AM.II.J.S3	Troubleshoot and repair aircraft fuel system.
AM.II.J.S4	Inspect a fuel selector valve.
AM.II.J.S5	Inspect and check manually-operated fuel valves for proper operation and leaks.
AM.II.J.S6	Troubleshoot a fuel valve problem.
AM.II.J.S7	Drain fuel system sump(s).
AM.II.J.S8	Service a fuel system strainer.
AM.II.J.S9	Inspect a fuel quantity indicating system.
AM.II.J.S10	Locate fuel system operating instructions.
AM.II.J.S11	Locate fuel system inspection procedures.
AM.II.J.S12	Locate fuel system crossfeed procedures.
AM.II.J.S13	Locate fuel system required placards.
AM.II.J.S14	Locate fuel system defueling procedures.
AM.II.J.S15	Troubleshoot fuel pressure warning system.
AM.II.J.S16	Locate troubleshooting procedures for fuel temperature systems.
AM.II.J.S17	Remove and install a fuel quantity transmitter.
AM.II.J.S18	Troubleshoot fuel quantity indicating system.

II. Airframe

Subject K. Aircraft Electrical Systems

References	*AC 43.13-1; FAA-H-8083-31*
Objective	*The following knowledge, risk management, and skill elements are required for aircraft electrical systems.*

Knowledge	The applicant demonstrates understanding of:
AM.II.K.K1	Generators, DC generation systems, and DC power distribution systems.
AM.II.K.K2	Alternators, AC generation systems, and AC power distribution systems.
AM.II.K.K3	Starter generators.
AM.II.K.K4	constant speed drive (CSD) and integrated drive generator (IDG) systems and components.
AM.II.K.K5	Voltage regulators and over-volt and overcurrent protection.
AM.II.K.K6	Inverter systems.
AM.II.K.K7	Aircraft wiring sizes, types, selection, installation and circuit protection devices.
AM.II.K.K8	Derating factors in switch selection.
AM.II.K.K9	Aircraft wiring shielding.
AM.II.K.K10	Aircraft lightning protection.
AM.II.K.K11	Instrument or instrument panel removal and installation.
AM.II.K.K12	Aircraft lighting systems.
AM.II.K.K13	Electrical system troubleshooting.
AM.II.K.K14	Soldering preparation, types of solder, and flux usage.
AM.II.K.K15	Aircraft electrical connectors, splices, terminals, and switches.
AM.II.K.K16	Electrical system measurement, adjustment, and testing.
AM.II.K.K17	Aircraft battery troubleshooting and maintenance.

Risk Management	The applicant demonstrates the ability to identify, assess, and mitigate risks associated with:
AM.II.K.R1	Testing/troubleshooting electrical systems or components.
AM.II.K.R2	Connecting or disconnecting external power.
AM.II.K.R3	Maintenance on energized circuits/systems.
AM.II.K.R4	Maintenance in areas containing aircraft wiring.
AM.II.K.R5	Routing and securing wires and wire bundles.
AM.II.K.R6	Selecting the size of wire in an electrical circuit.
AM.II.K.R7	Selection or installation of wire terminals.
AM.II.K.R8	Effects of soldering.
AM.II.K.R9	Soldering practices.

Skills	The applicant demonstrates the ability to:
AM.II.K.S1	Inspect aircraft wiring to verify installation and routing.
AM.II.K.S2	Perform wire terminating and splicing.
AM.II.K.S3	Assemble an aircraft electrical connector.
AM.II.K.S4	Use a wiring circuit diagram to identify components.
AM.II.K.S5	Solder aircraft wiring.
AM.II.K.S6	Troubleshoot an airframe electrical circuit.

AM.II.K.S7	Install airframe electrical wiring, switches, or protective devices.
AM.II.K.S8	Secure wire bundles.
AM.II.K.S9	Determine an electrical load in a given aircraft system.
AM.II.K.S10	Install bonding jumpers.
AM.II.K.S11	Check output voltage of a DC generator.
AM.II.K.S12	Check the resistance of an electrical system component.
AM.II.K.S13	Inspect generator brush serviceability and brush spring tension.
AM.II.K.S14	Inspect and check anti-collision, position, and landing lights for proper operation.
AM.II.K.S15	Inspect components in an electrical system.
AM.II.K.S16	Troubleshoot a DC electrical system supplied by an AC electrical system.
AM.II.K.S17	Identify components in an electrical schematic where AC is rectified to a DC voltage.
AM.II.K.S18	Perform a continuity test to verify the condition of a conductor.
AM.II.K.S19	Perform a test on a conductor for a short to ground.
AM.II.K.S20	Perform a test on a conductor for a short to other conductors.

II. Airframe

Subject L. Ice and Rain Control Systems

References	*AC 43.13-1; FAA-H-8083-31*
Objective	*The following knowledge, risk management, and skill elements are required for aircraft ice and rain control systems.*
Knowledge	*The applicant demonstrates understanding of:*
AM.II.L.K1	Aircraft icing causes/effects.
AM.II.L.K2	Ice detection systems.
AM.II.L.K3	Aircraft and powerplant anti-ice systems and components.
AM.II.L.K4	De-ice systems and components.
AM.II.L.K5	Wiper blade, chemical, and pneumatic bleed air rain control systems.
AM.II.L.K6	Anti-icing and de-icing system maintenance.
AM.II.L.K7	Environmental conditions that degrade vision.
Risk Management	*The applicant demonstrates the ability to identify, assess, and mitigate risks associated with:*
AM.II.L.R1	System testing or maintenance.
AM.II.L.R2	Storage and handling of deicing fluids.
AM.II.L.R3	Selection and use of cleaning materials for heated windshields.
Skills	*The applicant demonstrates the ability to:*
AM.II.L.S1	Inspect and operationally check pitot-static anti-ice system.
AM.II.L.S2	Inspect and operationally check deicer boot.
AM.II.L.S3	Clean a pneumatic deicer boot.
AM.II.L.S4	Troubleshoot an electrically-heated pitot system.
AM.II.L.S5	Inspect thermal anti-ice systems.
AM.II.L.S6	Inspect and operationally check an electrically-heated windshield.
AM.II.L.S7	Locate and explain the procedures for inspecting an electrically-operated windshield wiper system.
AM.II.L.S8	Locate and explain the procedures for replacing blades on a windshield wiper system.
AM.II.L.S9	Locate and explain the procedures for inspecting a pneumatic rain removal system.

II. Airframe
Subject M. Airframe Fire Protection Systems

References	*AC 43.13-1; FAA-H-8083-31*
Objective	*The following knowledge, risk management, and skill elements are required for airframe fire protection systems.*

Knowledge	*The applicant demonstrates understanding of:*
AM.II.M.K1	Types of fires and aircraft fire zones.
AM.II.M.K2	Overheat and fire detection and warning systems.
AM.II.M.K3	Overheat and fire detection system maintenance and inspection.
AM.II.M.K4	Smoke and carbon monoxide detection systems.
AM.II.M.K5	Fire extinguishing agents.
AM.II.M.K6	Types of fire extinguishing systems.
AM.II.M.K7	Fire extinguishing system maintenance and inspection requirements.

Risk Management	*The applicant demonstrates the ability to identify, assess, and mitigate risks associated with:*
AM.II.M.R1	Maintenance on circuits associated with fire bottle squibs.
AM.II.M.R2	Use of PPEs when working on or testing fire extinguishing systems.
AM.II.M.R3	Fire extinguishing agents.

Skills	*The applicant demonstrates the ability to:*
AM.II.M.S1	Troubleshoot an aircraft fire detection or extinguishing system.
AM.II.M.S2	Determine proper container pressure for an installed fire extinguisher system.
AM.II.M.S3	Identify maintenance procedures for fire detection and extinguishing system(s) and system component(s).
AM.II.M.S4	Inspect a smoke and toxic gas detection system.
AM.II.M.S5	Inspect a carbon monoxide detector.
AM.II.M.S6	Locate and explain the procedures for checking a smoke detection system.
AM.II.M.S7	Locate and explain the procedures for inspecting an overheat detection system.
AM.II.M.S8	Inspect fire protection system cylinders and check for hydrostatic test date.
AM.II.M.S9	Inspect fire detection/protection system.
AM.II.M.S10	Perform operational check of fire detection/protection system.
AM.II.M.S11	Inspect fire extinguishing agent bottle discharge cartridge.
AM.II.M.S12	Inspect a continuous-loop type fire detection system.

II. Airframe

Subject N. Rotorcraft Fundamentals

References	*AC 43.13-1; FAA-H-8083-31*
Objective	*The following knowledge, risk management, and skill elements are required for rotorcraft fundamentals.*
Knowledge	*The applicant demonstrates understanding of:*
AM.II.N.K1	Rotorcraft aerodynamics.
AM.II.N.K2	Flight controls.
AM.II.N.K3	Transmissions.
AM.II.N.K4	Rigging requirements for rotary wing aircraft.
AM.II.N.K5	Design, type, and operation of rotor systems.
AM.II.N.K6	Helicopter skid shoe and tube inspection.
AM.II.N.K7	Rotor blade functions and construction.
AM.II.N.K8	Rotor vibrations, track, and balance.
AM.II.N.K9	Drive system vibrations and inspection.
Risk Management	*The applicant demonstrates the ability to identify, assess, and mitigate risks associated with:*
AM.II.N.R1	Working around helicopter blades during ground operations.
AM.II.N.R2	Ground-handling procedures.
AM.II.N.R3	Ground operations and functional tests.
AM.II.N.R4	Maintenance and inspection of rotorcraft systems and components.
Skills	*The applicant demonstrates the ability to:*
AM.II.N.S1	Locate components of a helicopter rotor system.
AM.II.N.S2	Locate helicopter rotor blade track and balance procedures.
AM.II.N.S3	Locate and explain procedures needed to rig helicopter controls.
AM.II.N.S4	Locate and explain procedures to track and balance a rotor system.

II. Airframe
Subject O. Water and Waste Systems

References	*AC 25.1455-1, AC 120-39; FAA-H-8083-31*
Objective	*The following knowledge, risk management, and skill elements are required for water and waste systems.*
Knowledge	*The applicant demonstrates understanding of:*
AM.II.O.K1	Potable water system components and operation.
AM.II.O.K2	Lavatory waste system components and operation.
AM.II.O.K3	Inspection and servicing requirements for water and waste systems.
Risk Management	*The applicant demonstrates the ability to identify, assess, and mitigate risks associated with:*
AM.II.O.R1	Servicing lavatory waste systems, including use of safety equipment.
Skills	*The applicant demonstrates the ability to:*
AM.II.O.S1	Locate and explain the procedures for servicing a lavatory waste system.
AM.II.O.S2	Locate and explain the procedures for servicing a potable water system.

III. Powerplant

Subject A. Reciprocating Engines

References	*14 CFR part 43; AC 43.13-1; FAA-H-8083-32*
Objective	*The following knowledge, risk management, and skill elements are required for aircraft reciprocating engines.*
Knowledge	*The applicant demonstrates understanding of:*
AM.III.A.K1	Types of reciprocating engines.
AM.III.A.K2	Reciprocating engine operating principles/theory of operation.
AM.III.A.K3	Internal combustion engine operating principles/theory of operation.
AM.III.A.K4	Horizontally-opposed engine construction and internal components.
AM.III.A.K5	Radial engine construction and internal components.
AM.III.A.K6	Storage and preservation.
AM.III.A.K7	Reciprocating engine performance (e.g., PLANK, SFC).
AM.III.A.K8	Reciprocating engine maintenance and inspection.
AM.III.A.K9	Reciprocating engine ground operations.
AM.III.A.K10	Diesel engine operating principles/theory of operation.
Risk Management	*The applicant demonstrates the ability to identify, assess, and mitigate risks associated with:*
AM.III.A.R1	Maintenance that requires moving the propeller.
AM.III.A.R2	Preparation for and ground operation of a reciprocating engine.
AM.III.A.R3	Actions in the event of a reciprocating engine fire.
AM.III.A.R4	Use of other than manufacturer's procedures during maintenance.
Skills	*The applicant demonstrates the ability to:*
AM.III.A.S1	Perform a cylinder assembly inspection.
AM.III.A.S2	Operate and troubleshoot a reciprocating engine.
AM.III.A.S3	Install piston and knuckle/wrist pin(s).
AM.III.A.S4	Identify the parts of a cylinder.
AM.III.A.S5	Identify the parts of a crankshaft.
AM.III.A.S6	Identify and inspect various types of bearings.
AM.III.A.S7	Inspect and rig cable and push-pull engine controls.
AM.III.A.S8	Locate top dead-center position of number one cylinder.
AM.III.A.S9	Install a cylinder on a horizontally-opposed engine.

III. Powerplant

Subject B. Turbine Engines

References	*14 CFR part 43; AC 43.13-1; FAA-H-8083-32*
Objective	*The following knowledge, risk management, and skill elements are required for aircraft turbine engines.*

Knowledge	*The applicant demonstrates understanding of:*
AM.III.B.K1	Turbine engine operating principles/theory of operation.
AM.III.B.K2	Types of turbine engines.
AM.III.B.K3	Turbine engine construction and internal components.
AM.III.B.K4	Turbine engine performance and monitoring.
AM.III.B.K5	Turbine engine troubleshooting, maintenance, and inspection procedures.
AM.III.B.K6	Procedures required after the installation of a turbine engine.
AM.III.B.K7	Causes for turbine engine performance loss.
AM.III.B.K8	Bleed air systems.
AM.III.B.K9	Storage and preservation.
AM.III.B.K10	Auxiliary power unit(s).
AM.III.B.K11	Turbine engine adjustment and testing.

Risk Management	*The applicant demonstrates the ability to identify, assess, and mitigate risks associated with:*
AM.III.B.R1	Operation of a turbine engine.
AM.III.B.R2	Performing maintenance on a turbine engine.
AM.III.B.R3	Actions in the event of a turbine engine fire.
AM.III.B.R4	Foreign object damage.

Skills	*The applicant demonstrates the ability to:*
AM.III.B.S1	Identify different turbine compressors.
AM.III.B.S2	Identify different types of turbine engine blades.
AM.III.B.S3	Identify components of turbine engines.
AM.III.B.S4	Map airflow direction and pressure changes in turbine engines.
AM.III.B.S5	Remove and install a fuel nozzle in a turbine engine.
AM.III.B.S6	Inspect a combustion liner.
AM.III.B.S7	Locate the procedures for the adjustment of a fuel control unit.
AM.III.B.S8	Perform turbine engine inlet guide vane and compressor blade inspection.
AM.III.B.S9	Locate the installation or removal procedures for a turbine engine.
AM.III.B.S10	Locate and explain the procedure for trimming a turbine engine.
AM.III.B.S11	Identify damaged turbine engine blades.
AM.III.B.S12	Identify causes for turbine engine performance loss.
AM.III.B.S13	Inspect the first two stages of a turbine fan or compressor for foreign object damage.

III. Powerplant

Subject C. Engine Inspection

References	*14 CFR parts 43, 91; AC 43.13-1; FAA-H-8083-32*
Objective	*The following knowledge, risk management, and skill elements are required for aircraft engine inspections.*
Knowledge	*The applicant demonstrates understanding of:*
AM.III.C.K1	Inspection requirements under 14 CFR part 43 and 14 CFR part 91.
AM.III.C.K2	Identification of life-limited parts and their replacement interval.
AM.III.C.K3	Special inspections.
AM.III.C.K4	Use of FAA-approved data.
AM.III.C.K5	Compliance with service letters, service bulletins, instructions for continued airworthiness, ADs, or TCDSs.
AM.III.C.K6	Maintenance recordkeeping requirements under 14 CFR part 43.
AM.III.C.K7	Engine component inspection, checking, and servicing.
AM.III.C.K8	Engine mounts, mounting hardware, and the inspection and checking of each.
Risk Management	*The applicant demonstrates the ability to identify, assess, and mitigate risks associated with:*
AM.III.C.R1	A compression test on a reciprocating engine.
AM.III.C.R2	Maintenance on an operating reciprocating engine.
AM.III.C.R3	Maintenance on an operating turbine engine.
Skills	*The applicant demonstrates the ability to:*
AM.III.C.S1	Perform a compression check on a cylinder.
AM.III.C.S2	Evaluate powerplant for compliance with FAA-approved or manufacturer data.
AM.III.C.S3	Perform a powerplant records inspection.
AM.III.C.S4	Inspect for compliance with applicable ADs.
AM.III.C.S5	Determine engine installation eligibility.
AM.III.C.S6	Determine compliance with engine specifications, TCDS, or engine listings.
AM.III.C.S7	Perform a portion of a required inspection on an engine.
AM.III.C.S8	Check engine controls for proper operation and adjustment.
AM.III.C.S9	Inspect an engine for leaks after performing maintenance.
AM.III.C.S10	Inspect an aircraft engine accessory for serviceability.
AM.III.C.S11	Inspect engine records for time or cycles on life-limited parts.
AM.III.C.S12	Perform an engine start and inspect engine operational parameters.
AM.III.C.S13	Perform a portion of a 100-hour inspection on an engine in accordance with part 43.
AM.III.C.S14	Inspect an engine mount to determine serviceability.

III. Powerplant

Subject D. Engine Instrument Systems

References	AC 43.13-1; FAA-H-8083-32
Objective	The following knowledge, risk management, and skill elements are required for aircraft engine instrument systems.
Knowledge	The applicant demonstrates understanding of:
AM.III.D.K1	Fuel flow.
AM.III.D.K2	Temperature (e.g., exhaust gas, oil, oil cylinder head, turbine inlet).
AM.III.D.K3	Engine speed indicating systems.
AM.III.D.K4	Pressure (e.g., air, fuel, manifold, oil).
AM.III.D.K5	Annunciator indicating systems (e.g., warning, caution, and advisory lights).
AM.III.D.K6	Torquemeters.
AM.III.D.K7	Engine pressure ratio (EPR).
AM.III.D.K8	Engine indicating and crew alerting system (EICAS).
AM.III.D.K9	Digital engine control module (e.g., full authority digital engine controls (FADEC)).
AM.III.D.K10	Electronic centralized aircraft monitor (ECAM).
AM.III.D.K11	Engine instrument range markings and instrument conditions.
Risk Management	The applicant demonstrates the ability to identify, assess, and mitigate risks associated with:
AM.III.D.R1	Maintenance damage to the instrument or indicating system.
AM.III.D.R2	Engine instrument calibration or instrument error.
Skills	The applicant demonstrates the ability to:
AM.III.D.S1	Troubleshoot an engine oil temperature/pressure instrument system.
AM.III.D.S2	Troubleshoot a low fuel pressure indicating system.
AM.III.D.S3	Remove, inspect, and install a fuel-flow transmitter.
AM.III.D.S4	Remove, inspect, and install fuel-flow gauge.
AM.III.D.S5	Identify components of an electric tachometer system.
AM.III.D.S6	Check fuel-flow transmitter power supply.
AM.III.D.S7	Inspect tachometer markings for accuracy.
AM.III.D.S8	Perform resistance measurements of thermocouple indication system.
AM.III.D.S9	Remove, inspect, and install turbine engine exhaust gas temperature (EGT) component.
AM.III.D.S10	Locate procedures for troubleshooting a turbine EPR system.
AM.III.D.S11	Troubleshoot a tachometer system.
AM.III.D.S12	Replace a cylinder head temperature thermocouple.
AM.III.D.S13	Inspect EGT probes.
AM.III.D.S14	Locate and inspect engine low fuel pressure warning system components.
AM.III.D.S15	Check aircraft engine manifold pressure gauge for proper operation.
AM.III.D.S16	Inspect a manifold pressure system.
AM.III.D.S17	Repair a low oil pressure warning system.
AM.III.D.S18	Troubleshoot an EGT indicating system.
AM.III.D.S19	Inspect an oil temperature probe.

III. Powerplant
Subject E. Engine Fire Protection Systems

References	AC 43.13-1; FAA-H-8083-32
Objective	The following knowledge, risk management, and skill elements are required for aircraft engine fire protection systems.
Knowledge	The applicant demonstrates understanding of:
AM.III.E.K1	Types of fires and engine fire zones.
AM.III.E.K2	Fire detection warning system operation.
AM.III.E.K3	Fire detection system maintenance and inspection requirements.
AM.III.E.K4	Fire extinguishing agents, types of systems, and operation.
AM.III.E.K5	Fire extinguishing system maintenance and inspection.
Risk Management	The applicant demonstrates the ability to identify, assess, and mitigate risks associated with:
AM.III.E.R1	Container discharge cartridges.
AM.III.E.R2	Extinguishing agents.
AM.III.E.R3	Maintenance on circuits associated with electrically-activated container discharge cartridges (squibs).
Skills	The applicant demonstrates the ability to:
AM.III.E.S1	Troubleshoot and repair an engine fire detection system.
AM.III.E.S2	Identify fire detection sensing units.
AM.III.E.S3	Inspect fire detection continuous loop system.
AM.III.E.S4	Inspect fire detection thermal switch or thermocouple system.
AM.III.E.S5	Locate troubleshooting procedures for a fire detection system.
AM.III.E.S6	Inspect engine fire extinguisher system blowout plugs.
AM.III.E.S7	Inspect a turbine engine fire extinguisher container.
AM.III.E.S8	Inspect fire extinguisher discharge circuit.
AM.III.E.S9	Troubleshoot and repair a fire extinguishing system.
AM.III.E.S10	Inspect a fire extinguisher container discharge cartridge (squib).
AM.III.E.S11	Inspect fire extinguisher container and determine hydrostatic test requirements.
AM.III.E.S12	Inspect flame detectors for operation.
AM.III.E.S13	Check operation of fire warning press-to-test and troubleshoot faults.
AM.III.E.S14	Identify continuous-loop fire detection system components.

III. Powerplant

Subject F. Engine Electrical Systems

References	AC 43.13-1; FAA-H-8083-30, FAA-H-8083-32
Objective	The following knowledge, risk management, and skill elements are required for aircraft engine electrical systems.

Knowledge	The applicant demonstrates understanding of:
AM.III.F.K1	Generators.
AM.III.F.K2	Alternators.
AM.III.F.K3	Starter generators.
AM.III.F.K4	Voltage regulators and overvoltage and overcurrent protection.
AM.III.F.K5	DC generation systems.
AM.III.F.K6	AC generation systems.
AM.III.F.K7	The procedure for locating the correct electrical cable/wire size needed to fabricate a cable/wire.
AM.III.F.K8	The purpose and procedure for paralleling a dual-generator electrical system.
AM.III.F.K9	CSD and IDG systems and components.
AM.III.F.K10	Engine electrical wiring, switches, and protective devices.

Risk Management	The applicant demonstrates the ability to identify, assess, and mitigate risks associated with:
AM.III.F.R1	Polarity when performing electrical system maintenance.
AM.III.F.R2	Actions in response to a warning or caution annunciator light.
AM.III.F.R3	Maintenance on energized aircraft circuits/systems.
AM.III.F.R4	Routing and security of wiring near flammable fluid lines.

Skills	The applicant demonstrates the ability to:
AM.III.F.S1	Inspect engine electrical wiring, switches, and protective devices.
AM.III.F.S2	Determine suitability of a replacement component by part number.
AM.III.F.S3	Replace an engine-driven generator or alternator.
AM.III.F.S4	Inspect an engine-driven generator or alternator in accordance with manufacturer's instructions.
AM.III.F.S5	Troubleshoot an aircraft electrical generating system.
AM.III.F.S6	Remove and install an engine direct-drive electric starter.
AM.III.F.S7	Troubleshoot a direct-drive electric starter system.
AM.III.F.S8	Inspect an electrical system cable.
AM.III.F.S9	Determine wire size for engine electrical system.
AM.III.F.S10	Repair a broken engine electrical system wire.
AM.III.F.S11	Replace a wire bundle lacing.
AM.III.F.S12	Troubleshoot an electrical system using a schematic or wiring diagram.
AM.III.F.S13	Fabricate a bonding jumper.
AM.III.F.S14	Inspect a turbine engine starter generator.
AM.III.F.S15	Inspect engine electrical connectors.

Subject G. Engine Lubrication Systems

References	*AC 43.13-1; FAA-H-8083-32*
Objective	*The following knowledge, risk management, and skill elements are required for aircraft engine lubrication systems.*
Knowledge	*The applicant demonstrates understanding of:*
AM.III.G.K1	Types, grades, and uses of engine oil.
AM.III.G.K2	Lubrication system operation and components.
AM.III.G.K3	Wet-sump system.
AM.III.G.K4	Dry-sump system.
AM.III.G.K5	Chip detectors.
AM.III.G.K6	Lubrication system maintenance, inspection, servicing, and analysis.
AM.III.G.K7	Excessive aircraft engine oil consumption.
Risk Management	*The applicant demonstrates the ability to identify, assess, and mitigate risks associated with:*
AM.III.G.R1	Use or mixing of engine oils.
AM.III.G.R2	Following other than manufacturer's recommendations regarding the use of engine lubricants.
AM.III.G.R3	Handling, storage, and disposal of used lubricating oil.
Skills	*The applicant demonstrates the ability to:*
AM.III.G.S1	Inspect an oil cooler or oil lines.
AM.III.G.S2	Determine the correct type of oil for a specific engine.
AM.III.G.S3	Identify turbine engine oil filter bypass indicator.
AM.III.G.S4	Determine approved oils for different climatic temperatures.
AM.III.G.S5	Locate procedures for obtaining oil samples.
AM.III.G.S6	Inspect an oil filter or screen.
AM.III.G.S7	Perform oil pressure adjustment.
AM.III.G.S8	Identify oil system components.
AM.III.G.S9	Replace an oil system component.
AM.III.G.S10	Identify oil system flow.
AM.III.G.S11	Troubleshoot an engine oil pressure malfunction.
AM.III.G.S12	Troubleshoot an engine oil temperature system.
AM.III.G.S13	Identify types of metal found in an oil filter.
AM.III.G.S14	Remove and inspect an engine chip detector.

III. Powerplant

Subject H. Ignition and Starting Systems

References	*AC 43.13-1; FAA-H-8083-32*
Objective	*The following knowledge, risk management, and skill elements are required for aircraft ignition and starting systems.*
Knowledge	*The applicant demonstrates understanding of:*
AM.III.H.K1	Ignition system theory.
AM.III.H.K2	Spark plug theory.
AM.III.H.K3	Shower of sparks and impulse coupling.
AM.III.H.K4	Three electrical circuits of a magneto system.
AM.III.H.K5	Solid-state ignition systems.
AM.III.H.K6	Digital engine control module (e.g., FADEC).
AM.III.H.K7	Engine starters.
AM.III.H.K8	Magneto system components and operation.
AM.III.H.K9	Turbine engine ignition systems.
Risk Management	*The applicant demonstrates the ability to identify, assess, and mitigate risks associated with:*
AM.III.H.R1	Advanced and retarded ignition timing (piston engine).
AM.III.H.R2	Maintenance on engines with capacitor discharge ignition systems.
AM.III.H.R3	Working around reciprocating engines with an ungrounded magneto.
Skills	*The applicant demonstrates the ability to:*
AM.III.H.S1	Set magneto internal timing.
AM.III.H.S2	Time magneto to engine.
AM.III.H.S3	Remove, clean, and install spark plug.
AM.III.H.S4	Troubleshoot and repair an ignition system.
AM.III.H.S5	Inspect an electrical starting system.
AM.III.H.S6	Inspect magneto breaker points.
AM.III.H.S7	Inspect an ignition harness.
AM.III.H.S8	Inspect a magneto impulse coupling.
AM.III.H.S9	Troubleshoot an electrical starting system.
AM.III.H.S10	Troubleshoot ignition switch circuit.
AM.III.H.S11	Inspect and check gap of spark plugs.
AM.III.H.S12	Identify the correct spark plugs used for replacement installation.
AM.III.H.S13	Troubleshoot a turbine or reciprocating engine ignition system.
AM.III.H.S14	Identify the correct igniter plug and replace turbine engine igniter plugs.
AM.III.H.S15	Troubleshoot turbine engine igniters.
AM.III.H.S16	Inspect turbine engine ignition system.
AM.III.H.S17	Inspect igniters.

III. Powerplant

Subject I. Engine Fuel and Fuel Metering Systems

References	*AC 43.13-1; FAA-H-8083-32*
Objective	*The following knowledge, risk management, and skill elements are required for engine fuel and fuel metering systems.*
Knowledge	*The applicant demonstrates understanding of:*
AM.III.I.K1	Fuel/air ratio and fuel metering, and carburetor theory and operation.
AM.III.I.K2	Float carburetor theory, components, operation, and adjustment.
AM.III.I.K3	Pressure carburetor theory, operation, and adjustment.
AM.III.I.K4	Continuous-flow fuel injection theory, components, operation, troubleshooting and adjustment.
AM.III.I.K5	Digital engine control module (e.g., FADEC).
AM.III.I.K6	Hydromechanical fuel control system design and components.
AM.III.I.K7	Fuel nozzles and manifolds design, operation, and maintenance.
AM.III.I.K8	Components, theory, and operation of turbine engine fuel metering system.
AM.III.I.K9	Inspection requirements for an engine fuel system.
AM.III.I.K10	Fuel system operation.
AM.III.I.K11	Fuel heaters.
AM.III.I.K12	Fuel lines.
AM.III.I.K13	Fuel pumps.
AM.III.I.K14	Fuel valves.
AM.III.I.K15	Fuel filters.
AM.III.I.K16	Engine fuel drains.
Risk Management	*The applicant demonstrates the ability to identify, assess, and mitigate risks associated with:*
AM.III.I.R1	Adjusting a turbine engine fuel control.
AM.III.I.R2	Adjusting reciprocating engine fuel control systems.
AM.III.I.R3	Handling of fuel metering system components that may contain fuel.
AM.III.I.R4	Considerations during fuel system maintenance.
AM.III.I.R5	Handling of engine fuel control units that may contain fuel.
Skills	*The applicant demonstrates the ability to:*
AM.III.I.S1	Inspect, troubleshoot, and repair a continuous-flow fuel injection system.
AM.III.I.S2	Remove, inspect, and install a turbine engine fuel nozzle.
AM.III.I.S3	Identify carburetor components.
AM.III.I.S4	Identify fuel and air flow through a float-type carburetor.
AM.III.I.S5	Remove and install a carburetor main metering jet.
AM.III.I.S6	Inspect a carburetor fuel inlet screen.
AM.III.I.S7	Adjust a continuous-flow fuel injection system.
AM.III.I.S8	Inspect the needle, seat, and float level on a float-type carburetor.
AM.III.I.S9	Remove and install a float-type carburetor.
AM.III.I.S10	Adjust carburetor idle speed and mixture.
AM.III.I.S11	Locate procedures for a turbine engine revolutions per minute (rpm) overspeed inspection.

AM.III.I.S12	Inspect fuel metering cockpit controls for proper adjustment.
AM.III.I.S13	Locate procedures for adjusting a hydromechanical fuel control unit.
AM.III.I.S14	Locate and explain procedures for removing and installing a turbine engine fuel control unit.
AM.III.I.S15	Identify components of an engine fuel system.
AM.III.I.S16	Remove and install an engine-driven fuel pump.
AM.III.I.S17	Inspect a remotely-operated fuel valve for proper operation.
AM.III.I.S18	Locate and identify fuel selector placards.
AM.III.I.S19	Inspect a main fuel filter assembly for leaks.
AM.III.I.S20	Inspect fuel boost pump.
AM.III.I.S21	Locate and identify a turbine engine fuel heater.
AM.III.I.S22	Inspect fuel pressure warning light function.
AM.III.I.S23	Adjust fuel pump fuel pressure.
AM.III.I.S24	Inspect engine fuel system fluid lines and components.
AM.III.I.S25	Troubleshoot abnormal fuel pressure.
AM.III.I.S26	Locate the procedures for troubleshooting a turbine engine fuel heater system.
AM.III.I.S27	Remove, clean, and reinstall an engine fuel filter.
AM.III.I.S28	Troubleshoot engine fuel pressure fluctuation.
AM.III.I.S29	Inspect fuel selector valve.
AM.III.I.S30	Determine correct fuel nozzle spray pattern.

III. Powerplant

Subject J. Reciprocating Engine Induction and Cooling Systems

References	*AC 43.13-1; FAA-H-8083-32*
Objective	*The following knowledge, risk management, and skill elements are required for aircraft reciprocating engine induction and cooling systems.*

Knowledge	*The applicant demonstrates understanding of:*
AM.III.J.K1	Reciprocating engine induction and cooling system theory, components, and operation.
AM.III.J.K2	Causes and effects of induction system icing.
AM.III.J.K3	Superchargers and controls.
AM.III.J.K4	Turbochargers, intercoolers, and controls.
AM.III.J.K5	Augmenter cooling system.
AM.III.J.K6	Induction system filtering.
AM.III.J.K7	Carburetor heaters.
AM.III.J.K8	Pressure cowling air flow and control.
AM.III.J.K9	Reciprocating engine baffle and seal installation.
AM.III.J.K10	Liquid cooling system theory, components, and operation.

Risk Management	*The applicant demonstrates the ability to identify, assess, and mitigate risks associated with:*
AM.III.J.R1	Maintenance on turbochargers.
AM.III.J.R2	Ground operation of aircraft engines.
AM.III.J.R3	Maintenance-related FOD.
AM.III.J.R4	Chemicals used in liquid cooling systems.

Skills	*The applicant demonstrates the ability to:*
AM.III.J.S1	Inspect a carburetor heat system.
AM.III.J.S2	Inspect an alternate air valve for proper operation.
AM.III.J.S3	Inspect an induction system drain for proper operation.
AM.III.J.S4	Inspect engine exhaust augmenter cooling system.
AM.III.J.S5	Service an induction air filter.
AM.III.J.S6	Inspect a turbocharger for leaks and security.
AM.III.J.S7	Inspect and service a turbocharger waste gate.
AM.III.J.S8	Inspect an induction system for obstruction.
AM.III.J.S9	Inspect an air intake manifold for leaks.
AM.III.J.S10	Locate the proper specifications for coolant used in a liquid-cooled engine.
AM.III.J.S11	Inspect reciprocating engine cooling ducting (rigid or flexible) or baffle seals.
AM.III.J.S12	Identify components of a turbocharger induction system.
AM.III.J.S13	Identify exhaust augmenter-cooled engine components.
AM.III.J.S14	Inspect an air inlet duct for security.
AM.III.J.S15	Perform an induction and cooling system inspection.
AM.III.J.S16	Repair a cylinder baffle.
AM.III.J.S17	Inspect cylinder baffling.

| AM.III.J.S18 | Inspect cowl flap system for normal operation. |
| AM.III.J.S19 | Inspect cylinder cooling fins. |

III. Powerplant

Subject K. Turbine Engine Air Systems

References	*AC 43.13-1; FAA-H-8083-32*
Objective	*The following knowledge, risk management, and skill elements are required for aircraft turbine engine air systems.*
Knowledge	*The applicant demonstrates understanding of:*
AM.III.K.K1	Air cooling system theory, components, and operation.
AM.III.K.K2	Turbine engine cowling air flow.
AM.III.K.K3	Turbine engine internal cooling.
AM.III.K.K4	Turbine engine baffle and seal installation.
AM.III.K.K5	Turbine engine insulation blankets and shrouds.
AM.III.K.K6	Turbine engine induction system theory, components, and operation.
AM.III.K.K7	Turbine engine bleed air system theory, components, and operation.
AM.III.K.K8	Turbine engine anti-ice system
Risk Management	*The applicant demonstrates the ability to identify, assess, and mitigate risks associated with:*
AM.III.K.R1	Maintenance on compressor bleed air systems.
AM.III.K.R2	Ground operation of aircraft engines following other than manufacturer's instructions.
Skills	*The applicant demonstrates the ability to:*
AM.III.K.S1	Perform an induction and cooling system inspection.
AM.III.K.S2	Identify location of turbine engine insulation blankets.
AM.III.K.S3	Identify turbine engine cooling air flow.
AM.III.K.S4	Inspect turbine engine cooling ducting (rigid or flexible) or baffle seals.
AM.III.K.S5	Inspect a turbine engine air intake anti-ice system.
AM.III.K.S6	Identify turbine engine ice and rain protection system components.
AM.III.K.S7	Inspect a particle separator.
AM.III.K.S8	Inspect/check a bleed air system.

Subject L. Engine Exhaust and Reverser Systems

References	*AC 43.13-1; FAA-H-8083-32*
Objective	*The following knowledge, risk management, and skill elements are required for aircraft engine exhaust and reverser systems.*

Knowledge	*The applicant demonstrates understanding of:*
AM.III.L.K1	Reciprocating engine exhaust system theory, components, operation, and inspection.
AM.III.L.K2	Turbine engine exhaust system theory, components, operation, and inspection.
AM.III.L.K3	Noise suppression theory, components, and operation (e.g., mufflers, hush kits, augmenter tubes).
AM.III.L.K4	Thrust reverser theory, components, and operation.

Risk Management	*The applicant demonstrates the ability to identify, assess, and mitigate risks associated with:*
AM.III.L.R1	Maintenance and inspection of exhaust system components.
AM.III.L.R2	Operation of turbine engine reversing systems.
AM.III.L.R3	Operation of reciprocating engines with exhaust systems leaks.
AM.III.L.R4	Exhaust system failures.
AM.III.L.R5	Ground operation of aircraft engines.

Skills	*The applicant demonstrates the ability to:*
AM.III.L.S1	Identify the type of exhaust system on a particular aircraft.
AM.III.L.S2	Inspect a turbine engine exhaust system component.
AM.III.L.S3	Inspect a reciprocating engine exhaust system.
AM.III.L.S4	Inspect exhaust system internal baffles or diffusers.
AM.III.L.S5	Inspect exhaust heat exchanger.
AM.III.L.S6	Locate procedures for testing and troubleshooting a turbine thrust reverser system.
AM.III.L.S7	Perform a pressure leak check of a reciprocating engine exhaust system.

III. Powerplant

Subject M. Propellers

References	*AC 43.13-1; FAA-H-8083-32*
Objective	*The following knowledge, risk management, and skill elements are required for aircraft propellers.*
Knowledge	*The applicant demonstrates understanding of:*
AM.III.M.K1	Propeller theory and operation.
AM.III.M.K2	Types of propellers and blade design.
AM.III.M.K3	Pitch control and adjustment.
AM.III.M.K4	Constant speed propeller and governor theory and operation.
AM.III.M.K5	Turbine engine propeller reverse/beta range operation.
AM.III.M.K6	Propeller servicing, maintenance, and inspection requirements.
AM.III.M.K7	Procedures for removal and installation of a propeller.
AM.III.M.K8	Propeller TCDS.
AM.III.M.K9	Propeller synchronization systems.
AM.III.M.K10	Propeller ice control systems.
Risk Management	*The applicant demonstrates the ability to identify, assess, and mitigate risks associated with:*
AM.III.M.R1	Ground operation.
AM.III.M.R2	Propeller maintenance and inspections.
Skills	*The applicant demonstrates the ability to:*
AM.III.M.S1	Remove and install a propeller.
AM.III.M.S2	Check blade static tracking.
AM.III.M.S3	Inspect a propeller for condition and airworthiness.
AM.III.M.S4	Measure propeller blade angle.
AM.III.M.S5	Perform a minor repair to a metal propeller blade.
AM.III.M.S6	Perform propeller lubrication.
AM.III.M.S7	Locate and explain the procedures for balancing a fixed-pitch propeller.
AM.III.M.S8	Adjust a propeller governor.
AM.III.M.S9	Identify propeller range of operation.
AM.III.M.S10	Perform a 100-hour inspection of a propeller and determine airworthiness.
AM.III.M.S11	Determine what minor propeller alterations are acceptable using the propeller specifications, TCDS, and listings.
AM.III.M.S12	Inspect and repair a propeller anti-icing or de-icing system.

Appendix 1: Practical Test Roles, Responsibilities, and Outcomes

Applicant Responsibilities

The applicant is responsible for demonstrating acceptable knowledge of the established standards for knowledge, skill, and risk management elements in all subjects appropriate to the certificate and rating sought. The applicant should use this ACS and its references in preparation to take the oral and practical test.

An applicant is not permitted to know, before testing begins, which selections from each subject area are to be included in his/her test. Therefore, an applicant should be well prepared in all knowledge, risk management, and skill elements included in the ACS.

The oral portion of the test consists of questions specific to the topics associated with the codes on the Airman Knowledge Test Report (AKTR) as well as additional questions that are randomly selected by the Mechanic Test Generator (MTG). During the Oral portion of the test the applicant is **not** allowed to use any reference material to answer the oral questions asked by the examiner. Applicants will need to demonstrate acceptable knowledge of the subjects missed on the FAA knowledge test. The practical portion of the test continues with questioning, specific to the projects being tested.

The practical portion of the test continues with practical questioning, specific to the projects being tested. The applicant is allowed to use reference materials to answer the practical questions that are asked while the practical portion (projects) of the test is being administered.

The practical (skill) portion of the tests are significant as they measure the applicant's ability to logically think and objectively apply their knowledge, while demonstrating the physical skills that enable them to carry out aircraft maintenance in a safe manner. Satisfactory demonstration of each skill tested is evidence the applicant meets the acceptable degree of competency for the certificate or rating sought.

All applicants demonstrate an approval for return to service standard, where applicable, and demonstrate the ability to locate and apply the required reference materials. In instances where an approval for return to service standard cannot be achieved, the applicant explains why the return to service standard was not met (e.g., when tolerances are outside of a product's limitations).

Evaluator Responsibilities

The evaluator asks the applicant to provide the AKTRs prior to generating the test planning sheet. All deficient knowledge areas, as indicated by the ACS codes on the AKTRs, are retested during the oral portion of the test. If the applicant scores 100 percent on the knowledge exam, the minimum number of questions are asked during the oral portion of the test.

The evaluator generates a complete test planning sheet to conduct the oral and practical test. The evaluator includes all the questions and projects obtained from the internet-based Mechanic Test Generator (MTG) at https://avinfo.faa.gov/DsgReg/Login.aspx. The MTG includes oral questions from the knowledge elements of the ACS to retest those topics missed on the FAA knowledge exams, as well as a minimum number of additional oral questions, and these should be asked during the oral portion of the test.

The MTG includes questions on the knowledge and risk management elements of the ACS, specific to the selected projects; and these should be asked, in context, during the practical demonstration portion of the test. The applicant is allowed to use reference material for those questions that are given as part of the practical demonstration portion of the test. The evaluator personally observes all practical projects performed by the applicant. The practical portion of the test includes an ongoing evaluation of knowledge and risk management, while evaluating the skill. The evaluator who conducts the practical test is responsible for determining that the applicant meets acceptable standards of knowledge and skill in the assigned subject areas within the appropriate ACS.

The evaluator should be aware that any information on the test that is in parentheses ( ) is additional or clarifying information. It is not expected that the applicant will recite all the information in parentheses however, it is acceptable as an alternative to what is stated in the answer. The applicant is allowed to use reference material for those questions that are given as part of the practical demonstration portion of the test. For this reason it is imperative that the examiner ensure that the oral and practical portions of the tests are kept separate.

The following terms may be reviewed with the applicant prior to, or during, element assignment:

1. **Inspect** means to examine (with or without inspection enhancing tools/equipment).
2. **Check** means to verify proper operation.
3. **Troubleshoot** means to analyze and identify malfunctions.
4. **Service** means to perform functions that assure continued operation.
5. **Repair** means to correct a defective condition; and repair of an airframe or powerplant system includes component replacement and adjustment.
6. **Overhaul** means to disassemble, clean, inspect, repair as necessary, and reassemble.

In the integrated ACS framework, the sections contain subjects, which are further broken down into knowledge elements (i.e., K1), risk management elements (i.e., R1), and skill elements (i.e., S1). Knowledge and risk management elements are also evaluated during the knowledge testing phase of the airman certification process. The evaluator administering the oral and practical test must not combine subjects/elements during testing.

Further information regarding the requirements for conducting a practical test is contained in the current revision of FAA Order 8900.1 or FAA Order 8900.2, as applicable.

Appendix 2: Safety

General

Safety is the prime consideration at all times. The evaluator and applicant should be alert for hazards while performing any maintenance or troubleshooting projects. Should any project require an action that would jeopardize safety, the evaluator will ask the applicant to simulate that portion of the project.

The evaluator ensures the applicant follows all safety recommendations/precautions while performing the assigned projects including, but not limited to, the following:

1. Approach to the project; proper information and tools; preparation of the equipment; and observation of safety precautions, such as wearing safety glasses, hearing protection, and any other required personal protective equipment (PPE).
2. Cleaning, preparing, and protecting parts; skill in handling tools; thoroughness and cleanliness.
3. Use of current maintenance and overhaul publications and procedures.
4. Application of appropriate rules, risk management, and safety assessments.
5. Attitude toward safety, manufacturer's recommendations, and acceptable industry practices.

The applicant should be aware that any disregard for safety is not tolerated and will result in a failure.

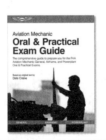